James T Lassell

The new South

or, Southern sentiments since the war

James T Lassell

The new South

or, Southern sentiments since the war

ISBN/EAN: 9783744737654

Printed in Europe, USA, Canada, Australia, Japan

Cover: Foto ©ninafisch / pixelio.de

More available books at **www.hansebooks.com**

A UNIQUE BOOK.

THE NEW SOUTH;

OR,

Southern Sentiment Since The War.

A Frolic of Fancy with Fact;

(*Embracing* SCENES *among the* CAUCASIANS, *and among the* NEGROES; VERDICT *of* JUSTICE; TRIUMPH *of* TRUTH; ERA *of* BROTHERLY-LOVE; STRICTURES *on* WAR; RELATION *of* THE "RACES;" &c., &c.).

BY
JAMES T. LASSELL, A. M.

PRINTED FOR THE AUTHOR.
JOHN MURPHY & CO., BALTIMORE.
1887.

COPYRIGHTED, 1887, BY JAMES T. LASSELL, A M.

DEDICATION.

To Politicians, to whose zeal there stand
Unnumbered monuments throughout our land
—*Low mounds*, beneath which lie the *marble* brows
Of myriads slain in war, and o'er which bows
The nation, *still*, in grief:
      To those in "grey"
And "blue," who, voice of duty, did obey;
Who left the dear ones and the joys of home
For country's sake—as each *viewed* "country"—come
What might:
    To those who patriotism *prove*
By pouring waters, from the springs of love,
On smould'ring embers of the section'l strife
Wherever found, till embers lose their life:

To votaries of Peace, throughout the world
Who would rejoice to see War swiftly hurled
From earth to realm, whence first he, raging, came
To lead the nations forth to deeds of shame :

To *all* these classes, he who undertook
To write for pastime, *dedicates* his book.
While to all those who have the taste and time
To read a strange eventful trip, in rhyme,
Presenting scenes where truth and fancy blend,
He would this poem, modestly, *commend*.

ENTERING UPON THE TRIP.

A Trip Through the South.

ENTERING UPON THE TRIP.

Like sated *Wolf* from mangled flock, *War* had from
    this, our torn
And bleeding, land retired: like *Shepherdess*, from
    flight forlorn,
Peace had returned, and entered on her office with
    success,
Leading the remnant of the flock afield with fond
    caress:
—Where crowded ranks of soldiers had been mar-
    shalled on the plains,
There stood great hosts—line after line—of shocks
    of various grains:
—Forgotten graves in which with haste the fallen
    had been thrown
On hill-sides bare, were hid by groves of oak and
    pine full-grown,

When to the South * again I rode on self-same steed
　　which bore
Me swiftly o'er its hills and plains, in troubled days
　　of yore
The "*Birth-Day of The Nation*" with its gladness
　　had returned ;
And grandsires told to children young true stories
　　they had learned
From fathers, buried "*years ago*," of battles which
　　were won
By "bare-foot soldiers following the noble Wash-
　　ington ;"
Of wondrous deeds of daring done, and sufferings
　　great endured,
By those whose blood and bravery had long ago
　　procured
For us the priceless blessings which our "*Independ-
　　ence*" yields ;
—As sowings bring the harvests that are garnered
　　from the fields.
The spirit of the "OLDEN TIME" was ev'ry-
　　where abroad ;
And, with that spirit, *actions* did, on ev'ry hand,
　　accord.
The old and young, both, gathered on that gala-day
　　in grove

---

*Reference is here made to a visit to the South during the War described in "*The Raid*" (unpublished).

Or shaded lawn to feast: and many a youth and
  maid there wove
With tender words and actions as the mystic warp
  and woof
A heart-bond strong of mutual love; while others
  gave a proof
(Agreed upon through glances) of a love confirmed
  and pure
By slyly joining hands beneath the flag with field
  azure
And galaxy of silver stars and stripes of white and.
  red
—Fit emblem of *strong union*—as it floated then
  o'er head.
At homes, too, there was feasting where glad yeomen
  and their wives
Well entertained companions of their early child-
  hood-lives.
The tear which came to matron's eye at thought of
  dear one dead,
Was brushed away before was e'en its tiny shadow
  shed
Upon the scene made bright with smiles by buoyant-
  hearted *joy,*
Whilst *panorama of the past,* did *Memory's* skill
  employ.
The country store and open space in front were
  occupied
By men and well-grown boys, who with

In word and deed of jest and sport; while all who
    passed that way
Received and gave back shouts of joy in honor of
    the day.
Old cannon were dug up from where they stood as
    hitching-posts
In towns, or borrowed at junk-shops, and dragged
    along by *hosts*,
With ropes, to vacant lots and fired, full-charged,
    while lying prone,
Amid loud shouts, the like of which, *by some*, had
    ne'er been known.
At well-selected spots within the shade, men, elo-
    quent,
And learned in various lore, with wit and fact and
    pathos blent,
Assembled multitudes engaged, amused, convinced,
    and moved
In patriotic speech, which *shouts* and *smiles* and *tears*
    approved.
The sound of gun in field and wood; the tonguing
    of the hound
Heard in the copse along the streams where fox and
    deer abound;
Full many anglers old and young, on bridges span-
    ning stream,
Or, in canoes staked at the spots where trout and
    perch did gleam
    …light, as to surface calm they oft did gayly

To gather food or take fresh air, or view the gorgeous
 skies
—These scenes and sounds attested well that sports-
 men used the day,
As one of special privilege to take all kinds of
 prey.
While thus on land and stream, at home, at public
 place, in field,
In grove, in grass-grown woodland path, and where
 the soil doth yield
To fawn's light tread, and harelets tremble at the
 wild-cat's voice,
Moved PLEASURE, clothed in Freedom's robe, and
 cried to all "Rejoice!"
The whir of evil angels' wings by ev'ry ear was
 heard;
And on each heart, all bright with joy, their shadows
 fell; and word,
Borne thro' the air from North which told those
 demons' mission dread,
Affrighted PLEASURE, who though robed in "*Stars
 and Stripes*," quick fled!
Pale *Consternation* swiftly came, and with her magic
 wand
Touched ev'ry brow and chilled the blood of all
 within that land.
As browsing doe and sportive fawn, far down within
 the brake,
Bewildered at the locomotive's shriek do start and
 quake;

As husbandmen receive the signs of coming summer-
    storm;
As woodman lone, in forest views a stranger's lifeless
    form;
As sleeping townsmen look abroad when 'roused by
    cry of "*Fire!*";
As young man hears an insult offered to an aged sire;
So—*variously*—the Southrons heard, upon that gala-
    day,
The sudden news that Garfield, *Head of this great
    nation*, lay
A-dying at the Capitol of deep and painful wound
Inflicted by a skulking foe who shot him to the
    ground.
"*The news*" became absorbing theme of all, both
    old and young;
And wrathful words were freely spoke by many a
    trenchant tongue.
But *one*, alone, of all I heard in careless manner
    spoke,
—And he was born on *Northern soil*—whose lan-
    guage did provoke
Contempt in all, and 'roused to wrath a score or more
    of those
Who erst had met on bloody fields, *brave* northern
    men as foes.
Among the "score" a princely man whose counte-
    nance did glow
With righteous ire, replied in words which swift
    and smooth did flow,

And with inherent, sparkling, heat did brightly,
    fiercely burn
—Like stream of molten iron comes from moulder's
    pouring-urn;
He closed: "*The man, whose heartless speech you
    heard, has my disdain!*
—*Who feels no grief at this sad hour, could do the
    deed of Cain!*"
All efforts at enjoyment now were formal failures; so,
The multitudes went homeward (but they moved in
    large groups, slow,)
While yet the sun had gone beyond the zenith scarce
    a pace,
As he majestically rushed 'like strong man in a race.'*
—Whilst with a throng of strangers mixed
    With friends, I rode and thought,
    A spirit, which attends man oft,
    Approached; yet no one caught
The fanning of her well-trained wing
    Except myself alone
To whom she spoke with greeting kind
    And in most winning tone,
As with her hand she gently touched
    My brow: "Canst thou not see
Throughout this land the wondrous scenes
    Which plain appear to me?"
"My vision is enlarged," I said,
    In softly whispered word,

* Psalm xiv.

And *started*, lest e'en that had been
 By some one overheard.
"What dost thou see?" she said, "Look well,
 For open to thy view
Are scenes such as no mortal eye
 Unaided, ever knew!"
"I see, I s-e-e," said I; but slow
 The words came from my tongue,
As all enrapt I gazed!—The ghosts
 Of those, both old and young,
Who had within that land once lived
 And died, for years agone,
Moving about and standing still
 In groups as men had done
Upon that day of gladness marred
 By sadness, plain I saw,
As mariner sees distant things
 Which close his glass doth draw.
Into the distance, first, I looked,
 As one upon tall peak
Will first the outer border scan
 Of landscape, ere he'll seek
The beauties and the wonders which
 On ev'ry hand lie near,
Because the field of vision doth
 So much enlarged appear.
My eye moved slowly, like the wave,
 (Which, safe, the sea-shell, bore
Wherein the infant *Venus* lay,)
 Moved t'ward Cythéra's shore,

When *Zephyrus*, with bated breath,
    Whispered to anxious *Deep:*
"I'll *gently* waft the tiny bark,
    So that your babe may sleep!" *
Or, like the shadow of a cloud
    On field of pasture moves,
When grazing flock, by walking, keeps
    The shade it so much loves,
And well discerned, when I looked *near*,
    Distinct in form and face,
The ghosts of many, I had known
    In flesh; and I could trace
The signs of sadness on each brow,
    And that, too, even while
Each looked with recognizing glance,
    And gave me friendly smile.
My *cicerone* bade me note
    That each ghost in right hand
Bore what appeared to be a staff
    Wrapped with a silken band.
"What do they bear in hand?" I said:
    "Those are their flags, close furled,"
Said she, "for *they, too*, feel the grief
    Which has on you been hurled.
Those ghosts, when first they heard (before
    The coming of the dawn)

---

* Mythology tells us that *Venus* was born of the *foam of the sea;* and was placed in a sea-shell which was wafted by Zephyrus to the island of Cythéra.

The boom of joy-guns and the sound
  Of huntsman's signal horn,
Although they had but late returned
  From rambling in the air,
Came eager from their graves again
  That they the joy might share
Of celebrating this great day
  Which had not for long years
Been greeted as, in olden time,
  It used to be, with *cheers.*
The flags they bear are photographs
  Of nature's lights and shades,
Bedecked with sparkles from the gems
  Which nightly crown the blades
Of grass that grow upon the graves
  Of soldiers, who with might
Contended, and who gave their lives,
  For *liberty* and *right!*
The staff on which each flag is set
  Was twig upon that tree
Which flourishes within this land
  —You, *by my aid,* can see
Its trunk and boughs which rise and spread
  To lakes and gulf and sea—
Shading and feeding ev'ry one
  —*The Tree of Liberty!*"
"O, look!" she cried, "there moves a group
  Of soldiers, dressed in '*grey,*'
Just as they fell! They far have come
  To be *at home* to-day.

Each has a small *Confed'rate* flag
  Full flying at his crest;
For while *that* flag above them waved
  They bravely sank to rest:
But, also, each bears in his hand
  A *Fed'ral* flag, close furled
In grief, for *that* flag would be *theirs*
  Were they *now* in '*the world.*'
Look! with them there is one in '*blue!*'
  —Far off in yonder wood,
He lay and died, but *when* or *why*
  Was never understood.
An angel-friend alone was near,
  (One that attends the brave,)
Yet strangers, (Southrons,) made for him
  Where he was found, *a grave!*
He has not visited *his home*
  Far in the northern-land
To-day; but staid, at warm request
  Of that Confed'rate band,
That he might be their honored guest
  As friend, nay *brother dear,*
And o'er the group, '*The Stars and Stripes*'
  —FLAG OF THE FATHERS!—bear!"
Just then I thought I felt hot breath
  Upon my cheeks; and turned
To see what friendly ghost had drawn
  So near; and well discerned
Imagination's shad'wy form
  Departing quick as thought!

'Twas *Reason's hand* that touched my cheeks
  And to them *burning* brought,
As he Imagination drove
  Away, and placed again
Before my eyes the veil which hides
  The world of ghosts, from men.
The friend who closest to me rode
  Was quick to catch the sight
Of *color* spreading o'er my face
  (—As doth the solar light
Flame at the East and spread o'er land
  And sea in golden flood,
When bright-eyed *Morn*, with cloudless brow,
  Greets *Earth* in cheerful mood—)
And asked me *where my thoughts had been,*
  That I should blush like maid?
"I feel no guilt; but I have seen
  A vision strange!" I said.
I felt cold tongues of paleness cross
  My brow, but not to stay
(—As polar lights gleam high, then low,
  Flash out, and die away—)
Whilst *Memory* the *present* changed
  To *past*, and plainly showed
War-scenes afresh!—But I was 'roused
  By sudden halt in road,
Made by the throng with which I moved
  (—As wind-mill-keeper wakes
From slumber deep, when sail-arms stop
  And mill no longer shakes.)

SCENE IN THE COURT OF A MANSION.

Beneath a tree of fol'age dense which stood within
  a court
Spacious, and ornamented with rich flowers of rarest
  sort
And shrubs indigenous and foreign sat an aged man
Reclining partly in a large arm-chair; whilst with
  a fan
A maiden cooled his brow—another fixed beneath
  his head
A pillow—and full oft was heard the question: "Is
  he dead?"
Uttered by persons on the outskirts of the multitude
That had just halted in the road through deep solici-
  tude
For welfare of the aged one, who tenderly was
  loved
By all, for, through a long, long life a grand man
  he had proved.
Dismounting I with difficulty moved among the
  crowd
Until I reached the court-gate, when I spoke my
  wish aloud:
"May we not come within the court, and gather
  close around
Our aged father in distress? We'll sit upon the
  ground,
If nearness to him while we stand, would be against
  his ease!"
"Come!" said the *aged sire*, "and *sit* or *stand*, just
  as you please!"

We entered as do worshipers into a temple go,
—Silent and solemn, moving, too, with lighten'd step
    and slow—
And took our places ev'rywhere within the spacious
    yard,
Not only in the gravel-walks, but on the grassy
    sward ;
On which we sat—the shawl or duster having first
    been spread.
Soon all were placed. The maid that fanned her
    sire then promptly said :
"Our father is quite feeble, having felt the heat
    to-day
To be exhausting; yet, he will attempt a word to say
To you who have such kindness shown and sympathy
    expressed
For him, as though he were by deadly malady
    oppressed."
The patriarch then raised his head ; and sat up—
    bust erect ;
And spoke in voice quite audible, in which we could
    detect
A tremor slight, yet musical, like *tremolo* in song
When wounded heart reviews and tells misfortune
    or deep wrong.

Speech of a Patriarch.

"Within a life of four-score years and eight,
Few days have dawned to me with joy so great

As this day dawned; and yet no deeper gloom
E'er hung, like shadow of some coming doom,
About my soul, than fell on me—*and you*—
Whilst yet the meadow grass was wet with dew!
But as in summer oftentimes a cloud
With vivid lightnings and with thunder loud,
Rises most darkling in the western sky
And with swift wings does o'er the heav'ns fly,
Pouring on earth huge urns of treasured rain,
Until the waters cover all the plain
And sending winds like giants fleet and strong,
Bent on destroying as they move along
Through field and forest, yet *that cloud retires*,
And leaves a clear sky ere the day expires;
So, dark foreboding for our cherished land,
—Caused by the wicked act of murd'rous hand
In slaying him who stood at head of State—
Which darkened all my soul, and havoc great
Made of the prospects for the South most rare
And growing hopes which I had watched with care
Planted by him who now lies in his blood
Has passed away and let an ample flood
Of comfort flow in full and radiant tide
From *that bright sun*—GOD'S PROMISE TO PROVIDE!"
"We of the South to troubles are inured;
—What could be *greater* than *we have endured?*—
And I have learned, *come ill from ev'ry hand*,
To trust to *God* the weal of this fair land!"
"The weal of man, or State, does not depend,
Always, on means employed to reach an end.

The end designed and means employed by men
May *both* be *wicked*, but 'tis true e'en then
That God will soon or late, bring good from ill
For those who are submissive to His will.
Wrong may prevail, and right be trodden down,
And justice flee before oppression's frown ;
Yet in due time some great good will be seen
Which would not, but for ill endured, have been.
Joseph was sold ; but from his selling came
A train of blessings which I need not name.
The negroes in this country have attained
To good they ne'er had known, had sires remained
In that dark land where even *to be free*
Is worse than living here *in slavery.*
We, of the *South*, have suffered cruel wrongs
From those who *stronger* were than we ; yet songs,
New songs, the lips of old and young employ
Because we, *since*, have found *new wells of joy !*
The unjust war against our liberty
Led to an act which made two races free
—Ourselves, who are of the Caucasian race,
And those who were our slaves, of sable face—
And now from lips of *both* rejoicings burst
At freedom from a slavery accursed
—A bondage, *theirs*, to outward act confined ;
A thraldom, *ours*, involving heart and mind.
Had we obtained what rightfully we sought
—A *peaceful separation*—then might naught
Of what we hoped to gain, have been our lot ;
While, in the years to come, will be forgot

The many cruel wrongs we have endured,
Amid prosperity and peace secured
By sealing in *firm union*, once for all,
These States, as *irons*, upon which doth fall
The welder's stroke, in *one* do close *unite*,
Though *line of union pass not out of sight!*"
" Nor did those noble men in battle slain
While fighting for our freedom, die in vain.
(—No! no! *ye shades!* 'twas not in vain ye fell,
Although the cause was lost, ye loved so well!
Ye and your country—The Confed'racy—
Have *passed away*, yet *live* in memory!—)
They will be on the page of hist'ry found
In future days recorded as *renowned*
For *gallant deeds*, in *just, defensive war!*
—The *loss of cause*, will *not their glory mar!*
The *old* flag, now above us, was, *by might*
Replaced whence it had been removed *by right;*
And yet we have experience to show
That to our peaceful homes more blessings flow
Than might have come 'neath that *new* flag we loved
When our dear sons on bloody fields well proved
Their courage, and devotion to that cause
Which all of us sincerely did espouse.
Hence, *now*, the *old flag* is, to us, more dear
Than e'er before the war it did appear;
And shall be ever o'er our land unfurled,
Till Doomsday's conflagration wrap the world!"
" Hence, thus I reason now : ' *The murd'rer's arm
Has brought us* ILL, *but not a* BLASTING HARM ;

A FIRE-BRAND.—(A Surviving "Rebel.")

If our Chief Magistrate may not survive,
His soul will safe at paradise arrive;
And on his widow, and dear children, all,
God's choicest blessings will abundant fall!'
—And oh! our land! *dear* land! MY *native* land!
Our *once dissevered, blood-cemented* land,
About whose borders, now, in many a band
The shades of thy departed statesmen stand
(—And heroes, and plain yeomen who have died—)
Anxiously watching thee as thou art tried
With this *new* fire, I *trust thee to our* LORD,
Who e'en *from fire* protection can afford!"
" Now my dear *children*—yes! for *thus* I *all*
Who are *much younger than myself*, do call—
Before you to your various homes repair,
Bring from yon staff that 'old flag,' floating there,
And wrap my aged form within its fold!"
While youths were gone for flag, " I'm *bold*,
Perhaps you'll think to speak a word
Suggested by what we have heard
Our aged father say," (spoke one
Who wore a sabre-scar upon
His finely formed, time-fluted, brow;
And who had lost sword-arm below
The elbow, from a bullet-wound
Received in war, where he was found,
At all times, at his post, and brave,—)
" There *was* a flag that *once* did wave
Above this land for which I feel
A love I wish not to conceal;

And *still* it floats in *mem'ry's sky*,
The FAIREST flag that e'er *did* fly!
Brave hands that flag defended well;
But, (sad the hour!) at last it fell!
Our hearts to give it up were loth,
For we lost *flag* and *freedom* both!
Why should JULY'S FOURTH DAY, *now, be
A joy to us*? *Our* FATHERS, FREE,
*Might well their ardent zeal employ,
In demonstration of their joy;
But what* THEY *gained at heavy cost*
—STATE INDEPENDENCE—WE *have lost!!*
Sad was the day when Gen'ral Lee
Surrendered! *We* should now be free,
And not compelled to do the will
Of Northern States—*that flag* would still
Be floating in this Southern air
As Freedom's emblem, true and fair—
Had he allowed his men to fight,
Who would have won at last despite
The heavy odds of ten to one
As they before, full oft, had done!
The cause that flag did represent
Was kindred to that which *you've* spent
This day in joyous words and deeds
To honor, notwithstanding *bleeds
Your President*, through deed late done
By ruthless hand at Washington.
Yes! cause of South was *Liberty
Of States*, as *Sov'reigns, to be* FREE!

That *cause* was torn as babe from breast
Of mother's torn by rav'nous beast:
That *flag* is buried like the form
Of mangled babe is hid from storm
And tempest and the cruel fangs
Of beasts and birds of prey, whilst hangs
Above it, from the bending sky,
God's just and ever watchful eye.
Well-watched by Him till 'Day of Doom,'
The *infant* then will come from tomb
And rise on wing high over beast
That tore it from its mother's breast:
That *flag*, too, the embodiment
Of cause which it did represent,
Though close entombed it sleeping lies
Will, yet, *with life immortal*, rise,
Changed in appearance and in name
But lifted from the earth by same
Pure spirit with which it was born,
And which it bore when it was torn
From fond embrace of her who gave
It birth—who striving it to save
Lost her own life and found her grave."
"As *resurrected babe* will be
From *special* claim of *mother* free
(—Though she will greet it in the sky
As *babe of hers in time gone by*—)
And by its presence bless the world
Of spirits pure, that *flag* unfurled,
—Appropr'ate garb of deathless cause—

Will, by all nations, with applause
Be hailed as angel sent to bless
This world; while, oft, in fond caress,
The *risen South*, with joy complete,
Her offspring *glorified* will greet,
—Though now she sleepeth, side by side,
With '*cause*' for which she lived and died!"
"Yes, *South is, as a nation*, dead;
But States still live in close bond wed
To *Union;* yet *that, too, will die*
In fast approaching by-and-by!
The States at North and East and West,
Will think it to their *interest*
(And, therefore, will not question '*right*'
For which they forced the South to fight
—Which *Massachusetts long did claim*
And threatened to demand, in name
Of her own *sov'reignty, innate,*)
From Union to separate!
When that day comes, *then* men will see
The Flag of the Confed'racy,
And *spirit of that truth it bore,*
Living again, TO DIE NO MORE!
"Then let the *babe* and *mother* sleep
Till *resurrection-day!* We'll weep
The tears of those whom *hope* doth cheer,
That *buried ones* will *yet appear*
In *recognized reality,*
And *clothed with immortality!*"
Thus *he:*—and *choral murmur* came

From *multitude;* whose cries, "*Oh! shame!*",
"*False-prophet!*", their *disfavor told.*

SPEECH OF A SOUTHERN YOUTH.

"*Old flag*" was brought. A *youth* cried: "Hold!
A moment, comrades, ere you place
The flag around our father! Brace
Yourselves and stretch its corners, four,
As tho' it still were floating o'er
Our heads, unrolled by joyous breeze
Which now is sporting 'mid the trees!
So!—Much of *all that has been said,*
Did sound like ancient language, *dead,*
(Which must be learned alone from *books,*)
To many here, as *plainly,* looks
Did show! The troubles of '*The South*',
We that are young, have heard at mouth
Of those who did 'the troubles' bear,
As stories told at times most rare.
—Our fathers, and our brothers, fell
In war: our mothers, tearful, tell
Their last adieu: 'With *life in hand*
We go, before our foes to stand,
And drive them back; but should we fall,
Let not our fate your hearts appal!
'Tis well to die defending home
Against invaders, fierce, who come!
Our *love* for *home sends us away,*
With hope that we'll return, some day.

Farewell ! Be *cheerful!* Though *we die*
In battle, there is *One on high*
In whom we trust—and *you*, as well—
We'll meet in heav'n ! Loved ones, farewell !'
—The '*blacks*' did once obedience yield
To '*whites*'; and served in house and field
As slaves. The '*South*' displayed a flag
As *nation new*, which '*North*' did drag
Down from its standard, after years
Of struggle, whilst *flowed blood and tears.*
These things we know as HISTORY !
And, *oft*, they seem like *mystery!*
We wonder how such things *could be*
Within this land so blest and free
As *we* now find it. That *War trode*
All o'er our land, *as episode*
Most wonderful we view
In life of nation now so true
And kind, *one* to *another*. We
The ' *Flag of The Confed'racy*
Have, not all, seen upon the air ;
Though *all*, perhaps, have been shown where
It *did once* float above the brave
Who fought and died the cause to save
Of which that flag was chosen sign :
(—About whose memories we twine
The chaplet due to *honor's* brow
And at whose graves we fain would, now,
Love's tender offerings renew
And sprinkle sorrow's pearly dew :—)

And *yet* that *cause* to *us* is known
As *cause* of *those now dead*, ALONE."
—"The *flag you have*, my comrades, *there*,
Has hearts of Southern youth: no share
Doth any other ensign hold
In our affections! Take it; *fold*
It 'round our father! It is meet
Both old and young that flag should greet
With loving touch! *Yourselves* enfold,
As well as *him*, with flag you hold:
And thus (with *heart to heart*, both *youth*
And *age* wrapped in that flag,) the TRUTH
Displayed in living grand tableau,
To our enraptured vision show!"

THE FIRE-BRAND QUENCHED.

'Twas grandly done as he did ask;
And—*but* my pen halts at the task
Of striving to describe the scene
Which then ensued!—The dancing sheen
Shed from the lightning's face doth come
Before no louder startling bomb,
Than rushed upon the air, in noise
Of pealing joy spoke by the voice
Of that vast multitude as though
A vocal hurricane did throw
Its vehemence in human tongue
Upon the quiv'ring ear! Among
The woods so *long* glad *echo* played

Her grand response on organ made
Of hill and dale with rock inlaid
—Its pipes all masked—that, quite dismayed,
Coy *Silence* fled across the land
Nor stayed her steps at ocean-strand!
The multitude renewed the shout;
When even those who bore about
Them war's rude marks in scar and maim,
Joined, joyously, in glad acclaim.
—Tableau well showed that *heart* and *hand*
Of all within the Southern-land
Attach to Union, whose flag's fold
Held in embrace both *young* and *old*.
They grasped the flag; and, each pressed heart
With its rich folds as if to part
With it would be, for them, like death
To joys more precious than their breath.
Short time elapsed : then youths did rest
The azure field with stars on breast
Of aged one ; and, stripes of red
And white about his form, save head,
(—That *wish* of *his* might nothing lack—)
They loosely wrapped ; and then stepped back.
He, THEN, stretched out upon his chair.
We watched him, calmly lying there,
While the breezes fingered his flowing white locks,
Which were soft as the fleece of *nomadic* flocks.
And, playing on his noble face,
A *smile* of pleasure we could trace.
—But he grew quickly *pallid;* and one, aloud,

Cried: "*The Flag of the Land has become his* SHROUD!"
Full many friends, with rapid stride
Approached the dying patriot's side;
And his trembling daughters whilst lifting his head
Made the *breezes* SHUDDER, by wailing: "HE'S DEAD!!"
As there he lay in death serene,
I recognized the "*Horseman*" * seen
At a mansion's gate when the famous "*Black Raid*"
Through that section in time of the war was made.
Some bore him away in '*the blue, white and red;*'
And office performed which was due to the dead.
While, slowly, t'ward '*home*' all the rest did repair;
First casting for *selves* and for *country* all care
On *Him*, who so *gently* from earth '*sire*' had led,
That SMILING, '*sire*' entered *the land of the dead!*

* "Horseman" was a character in "The Raid," an unpublished poem by same author.

SCENES AMONG THE COLORED PEOPLE.

SCENES AMONG THE COLORED PEOPLE.

By private roads digressing, (or by paths,
Which, like huge serpents, stretched on stubble fields
Were seen; else, winding through the standing maize,
Were hid from view,) the multitude, some here,
Some there, passed to their various homes; and I
Was left to travel whither my design
Might lead. The sun had trode well nigh three-
    fourths
His course from east to west, when I drew near
A grove of beech and oak, close to the road;
Where hundreds of the negro race had met
To celebrate the day in manner such
As each might think the best. I rode into
The grove, and being recognized by some
Who knew me in the days before the war,
Was well received with words of welcome warm.
I saw at once they had not heard "the news;"
For ev'ry face was lighted up with joy,

And ev'ry voice danced with delight in song,
Or speech, or laugh, which made the welkin ring,
And "woke up" Echo in the swamp near by.
Such speech! such *song!* such *frantic joy!* Did eye
And ear e'er *witness such—so strangely blent?*
Religious exercises were, by some,
Held where rude seatings had been improvised;
—There boiling exhortations were poured forth
From foaming lips; and men and women knelt,
And shook their bodies, and tossed their heads, and threw
Into the air wild words of joyous praise
And prayer, most vehement, which were to me,
Like errant birds of unknown land and wing.
Strange choruses concerning "Canaan's Shore"
And kindred themes, were sung, in rhythm unique,
By voices rich in melody, which rose
And fell and trembled in sweet harmony,
Expressing ev'ry chord in unison.
On outskirts of the grove, the *rustic dance*
Went on, to music wonderfully real,
Produced by skilful hand in playing harp
Of single string;* in "*patting Juba Ju;*"
Or thumbing wondrous *coon-skin banjer's* strings.
At one place stood a group entranced *by song*
—"Away down on the Swanee River, far
Away"—played on 'accordin' by one blind,
And sung by aged pair, whose home, in youth,

---

* Jew's Harp.

Had been upon the bank of that same stream,
And who, whilst slaves, in days long gone, had been
Brought northward (kindred being left behind.)
Their power of song was passing great; and whilst
They sang, they wept. When song was o'er the twain
Arose; and, in loud voice, the husband cried:
" *O bless de Lord! doe we did leab our home
And ole folks dar, dese many days ago,*
WE NOW IS FREE! *I's ready now to cross
To Can'an's sho'; I say, I'se* READY NOW
*Ou' fokes, to cross to Can'an's happy sho'.
O bless de Lord, I's glad to see dis day!
Hooray! fur Mr. Linkin, and de Fofe
Day of July!"* The wife then gave a scream
Of ecstacy; and straightway, she began
To sing a song whose sentiment did thrill
My being through—a song whose words have ne'er
Been set in type, nor writ—to which she joined
The chorus: " I am going home to die
No more;" in singing which the group gave aid
With zest. The blind man was of that old pair
The son—the only child; and sat with face
Upturned, and gazed abroad upon the sky
With sightless eyes, as if in search of light.

At still another part of that large grove
The violin (whose many voices seemed
To utter weird words of joy to charm
The ear of spirits who might dwell within
That ancient wood,) put into frenzy great

Of wild delight, which knew no bound or rule
Of meet expression, by or word or deed,
A crowd that numbered scores, both old and young,
Of sexes both.
                      And, yet again, at short
Remove from this last scene, *an orator*,
In phrase well suited to his audience,
Descanted on the glories of the land
We call our own; informing all who well
Attended to his words, that *Washington
Was born*, and many other great events
Had happened on the day which, then and there,
They all had met to celebrate with joy.
And *many facts*, he there made known which have
Escaped the notice of historians.
The orator was young: yet, few among
His hearers, thought his hist'ry was at fault,
Besides a grey-haired barber from a town
Remote; who promptly spoke, correcting *one*
Mistake as follows: " Friend, you's *jamb-by* right:
But teachers o' de people ought *to* KNOW
What dey is talkin' 'bout! An' wherefoe, friend,
I takes dis chance in order to obstruct
Yoe mind on dis one pint, as you is *young:*
De great George Henry Washington, 'bout who
We hears so little now-a-days, but whom,
When I was young, *was all the go, 'an den*
Was called de father of dis land, dat is
Of all the *people* in dis land, *bofe white*
And *cullud*—HE *warn't* BORND, *but den he* DIED

De fofe day of July in seventy-six;
Which fac' ou' childurn, *now* in school books learns;
And I has seen it, foe now, fur myself,
In Dicleration of Dependence, lent
Me by de jedge, who lives whar I live,
And *likewise gits* his shavin' done by me!
My friend, *amember* dis formation, when
You speaks de next time on a 'cashun like
De present. Take my word! On it *prelie!*
Fur it *is spoke by ole grey-headed Joe.*
My *marster knowed George Washington;* and *I
Knows what I say!"*—and then the old man laughed
In triumph; adding, most complacently,
"*Go on, my friend; I's done.*" The *orator*
Confessed himself corrected; and, at once,
Threw eulogistic flowers on Lincoln's grave.
Whilst I was lost in musings on the sad
Estate of those poor sons of Africa,
Whose heritage was mental feebleness,
And ignorance profound, *commotion filled
The grove*, like sudden rush of hurricane;
And wild cries pierced the air! Then groans, most
   deep;
And plaintive pleadings; shrieks of agony;
Ejaculation most devout, yet wild;
—Such voicings as most likely would be heard
In crowded streets of city, all ablaze,
Without a way of exit—struck my ear
And came in quick succession, like the taps
Of rolling drum: while tott'ring, stagg'ring forms,

As if in drunken reel ; and shaking heads ;
And hands held high, and quiv'ring like the tongues
Of fire do move; and close clenched fists, slow moved
In circle o'er the head ; and men and boys,
As well as girls and women, running to
And fro, *all* met my gaze where'er I turned.
The multitude was crazed, like flock within
A fold attacked by wolves; or, citizens
Unarmed and threatened with a massacre.
I knew "the news" had come, from words which
 rang
Distinct above confusion's cascade-roar—
Such words as these : "*O Linkin's shot agin!*"
*The President is killed! Dar's war dey say
In Washington, an' Mister Garfiel's shot!*"
"*Ou' time is come! We'll all be slaves! Farewell
To Liberty!*"; "*O hush! 'tis no sich thing!
I'll die, afoe I'll be a slave!*" "*Who says
He's shot? Who brought de news? Where is de man?*"
—Such words told plainly, that "the news" had been
Received, which I had closely kept from souls
So full of joy. The pain my own soul felt
At witnessing that scene of wild dismay,
Was such as *pity, fear*, deep *grief*, and *hope*,
Profound *regret* and ardent *wish*, and *wrath*,
Resolve, (both bold and strong,) curbed by *despair*
—And almost ev'ry impulse known to man—
Hard struggling for the mast'ry, could inflict.

But, suddenly, a lull in that fierce storm

Of grief and frantic dread, which had so whirled
The multitude, occurred; and then a calm
—Oppressive, painful, death-like, *perfect calm*—
Ensued, as at a spot of rising ground
Near centre of the grove, and standing straight
On bench of manufacture rude, but broad,
And firmly built, a tall, athletic man,
Of hoary locks, and furrowed face embrowned
With Afric's milder hues, stretch forth his hand
And waved to silence. " Who is he ?" I asked;
And learned, he was the preacher most esteemed
For eloquence among the " Colored Folks"
Throughout that section of the Southern land,
And called by ev'ry body "*Uncle Josh.*"
The waving hand dropped gracefully beside
The noble form ; and with a voice both strong
And great of compass—like the bugle's voice—
The preacher spoke :—his mien was kingly, (*grand !*)
His spirit, *love ;* his words were such as his
UNTUTORED mind had gathered, here and there,
Distorting many from their sound and sense,
As known to those who rightly speak our tongue :
" My brothren in de flesh, an' also in de faith,
I'm sensible o' pain, bofe deep an' sharp,
As I arise to 'spress my feelings here
On dis uccashun. Sad, indeed, in tone
And words, de woice which spoke to us jist now
From Washington ! It fell upon dese ears
Like news o' death, in my own family !
I felt like saying, 'Absalom, my son,

Would God that I had died instead of thee,
Son Absalom.'—The President is shot!
Dis makes de *second* time we's lost de head
O' dis apublic by his bein' shot!
The fust was Lincoln—sainted Lincoln—frien'
Of all the cullud race—yes, *he* were shot;
But when he died, his spirit tuck its flight
To that *ether'al* blue expanse of yon
Resounded wault of sublumary worls!
And now, on *Anniversionary-Day*,
When *Liberty* was bornd triumphant, *here*
In *dis great land*, the dreadful "news" has come
Dat Mr. Garfiel has been shot—dat friend
O' bofe de blacks an' whites—and breathed his last
Upon this transubstantial mundame spere,
Where wicked men brings trouble, but de good
And wary dey finds rest! It's sad to think
About! But shill we therefoe, now, subcum
To dis infliction o' de penulty
O' death upon our dear good Presedunt,
So universal common—yes, *to all*
De human family, from anciunt days,
When *'Thewslem riz* and *reigned* in Israel
And Jacob all his sheep and cattle watched
In fiels and woods, an' swamps of ole Judee;
And run de risk o' going from dis worl
Afoe ou' time, thew mere *egzitement?* NO!
Beloved brothrun, *do restrain yerselves!*
Keep cool! Why jist awhile ago, you all
Aminded me most strikingly o' poor

Pholipyan jailer, who was jist about
To kill hisself *thew great egzitement*, 'cause
De chains o' Paul and Cyrus were struck off
By Angel's hands; an' he, poor fellow, thought
Hisself asponsible fur what dey done!
But Paul cried: 'Stop! don't hurt yerself! De fault
Ain't yourn dat we has been sot free from chains!'
And so I would advise you all to-day:
Don't hurt yerselves because de mortal chains
Dat boun de Presidunt in dis dark worl
—Dis *prison* worl—has been ondone an' *he*
Has gone to dwell wid angels bright whar bofe
De bullit an' de pistol is onknown,
An' pain an' *death* kin never, never, come!
The jailer *minded* what de 'postle *told*
Him: so ought you to mind what *I* say *now!*
Be *joyful*, like you was befoe de 'news'
Had come! 'Tis not *your fault* de Presedunt
Were shot! 'Rejoice!' de 'postle says, 'an pray.'
I'd ketch the echo of his woice, and say:
'*Yes! let yoe joys aboun' thewout de day;*
Till yon bright sun goes home and 'fuses us
His comp'ny any longer in dis grove!'
Thar's some among ye, who has never learnt
To pray, perhaps; but, thar is no one here
Who kinnot sing, or laugh, and play. O, no!
For thar's a joy-spring in de black-man's heart
What always freely runs exceptin' pain
Or sickness do, like leaves or fallin limbs
O' trees, fill up de outlet ditch! Clar dese

Away, an' den de stream flows free again!
Thar never were a time when, as a race,
We cullud folks could not rejoice. De Jews
When in de Babylonium land, refused
To sing de hymns dey learnt at home; an' hung
Their harps upon de willer-tree; an' would
Not strike a string! But all de cullud fokes
Who lived in this great Southern land, when slaves
An' bearin' troubles hard as any what
De Jews did ever have, would sing de songs
O' Zion with a will—them what belonged
To church I mean; an' others sot their notes
To *cornfiel songs,* an' sich as suit de fokes
What go a courtin'. No one ever seen
A *banjer* or a *wiolin* down *here,*
Upon a tree, unless it were forgot
Er hid, or else de owner had got tired
O' playin!—*Cullud fokes! we's saw ou' share*
O' trouble; and we has a right to sing,
Er laugh (—I will not 'clude to dance—)
While we does sojourn in dis lower worl!
De Red Sea have been crossed! We crossed dry shod!
We's left ou' Egypt to ou' back! I know
We still is in de wilderness; but, Oh!
Clar water flows from rocks, an' manny falls
Bofe day and night; de quails can't help therselves,
But *must* keep comin' to ou' moving camp,
As we goes marchin' fur de stormy banks
O' Jordan, whar we stands and casts ou' eye
To Canaan's far an' happy land, whar ou'

Perzeshuns lie! O, brothrun, 'deed I feels
We has a right to gether in de grapes
De Lord has made to grow all 'round us here!
*Injoy yerselves, ye people free, on dis
De nation's holidays!* De great ones thar
At Washington, will do things as dey ought
To be. It won't do any good fur you
To scream an' cry, an' be afeer'd *o' what
Ye* DO NOT KNOW! *I* grieves as much as *you;*
But den *I's* got my *senses 'bout me too!*
What man were that who said, *'Dar's War agin?'*
War *whar? Twixt who? De North an' South?* I tell
Ye, friens, *thar never will be war agin
B·tween de two.* Dey bofe, like brothers who
Has fought, would jine an' whip mos' any man
Who'd try to make dem fight agin. De graves
Of soldiers who was killed are mos' too fresh
To 'low de white fokes in dis lan' to take
De field agin! An' den de widders made
By war within de lan', an' orphuns who
Still looks aroun' fur father; an' de men
Whose arms, an' legs, an' eyes, lies sum'ers long
De track whar war walked thew dis Southern-land
Mos' ankle deep in white men's blood, an' flung
De darts o' death from *bofe his hands at once,*
Would, with a mighty power of 'suasion rise
And plead aginst de rasin' of a war!
I fears no war! So much fur *dat one pint!*
But den, I heard a voice cry out; 'Farewell
To Liberty! We's now all slaves!' Dat cry

Were mos' anough to make an ANGEL come
An' comfort dat poor soul! But, ef he come
We did not see his shinin' robe, nor hear
De rus'lin' of his foldin' wings among
De vast disorder an' confusion what
Provailed thewout de grove. Yit I am nigh
Anough an angel, fur de task of quick
Convicin' dat dear frien' dat he is WRONG
In holdin' sich opinion on de great,
And sollum pint of liberty! Now, come,
My friend, who were it tuck de tremblin' hand
Of our poor race, an' put it in de hand
O' Liberty, an' said: 'I marry you
In bons o' mutu'l everlastin' love?
Did Mr. Lincoln? No! He beckoned all
Us cullud fokes to come away from home,
An' he would try t' effect for us a match
(Like what we calls down here a run-way match
When them what has control o' young fokes do
Not give their free consent that they may go
Git married.) Mister Lincoln could not speak
Fur us an' also Liberty: besides,
We could not git away to go whar sweet
Faced Liberty, with smile an' outstretched hand
Were waitin' patiuntly fur us to come!
Who made us free? agin I ask. Did War?
O no! my friends! Ef dat were so, den war
Mought make us slaves agin, some day! I know
Dat when de war were done, we stood beneath
De 'stars and stripes' upon dat glorious flag

What floats triumphant o'er dis Continent
(Like dat which have been hiested on yon pole
Out by de road,)—*the Flag o' Liberty!*
But den we stood dar 'foe de war, an' yit
Were slaves! But by-and-by dese wery States
—Ou' guardeens—*give consent* dat all us fokes
Might be united in a wedlock strong
To objict of ou' love; an' signed de bond
O' marriage contract thar in Washington!
I say, *we's wed by* LAW *to* LIBERTY,
De beautiful an' 'posin' bride fur whose
Fair hand ou' hearts did ache thew many long
An' wary years! De States—*mind all de States
O' dis Confedric Union*—*give consent!*
Den who kin give a *writin' of divorce
Betwixt us two?* NOBODY! *No!* No!! NO!!!
Not even WAR *with all his mighty strut!*
But lastly, dat is, *thirdly*, I inquire
Who made us free? which I will answer thus:
THE LORD! *'Twas He, alone, that made us free!*
When Moses heerd de Lord commandin' him
To bring his chosen people from de land
Of Egyp', did de leader 'spect to take
De credit to *hisself?* An' when he give
De inwitation to de people, were
It not de *inwitation* of *de* LORD?
When Pharoah said de people *dey mought go*,
Who brung about dat change in Pharoah's mind?
'*De miracles o' Moses*', you may say.
Who give de power to work de plagues? Dat's it!

The *Lord*, of course! So do we cullud fokes
Thewout de South *now wear* de shinin' *Badge
O' Liberty*, because the LORD *has put
It on us*, an' has tuck away de '*Yoke
O' Bondage*'! Bless de Lord, *its pinned upon
Us wid de golden clasp o' Gospel Love*,
What glitters wid de glorious light
Of revulation! And upon de face
O' dat bright clasp, is seen de *phomographs
O' Liberty* and *Man* (—and DAT man's *skin
Has all de colors in de alfubet!*—)
And at de bottom o' de clasp is writ :
'Them whom the Lord has jined, let no man put
Asunder!' Yes, my friens, de *Lord* has jined
De heart o' Liberty and ourn in love;
And jined ou' hands in wedlock, *which shill last
As long as we bofe live!*"—

"I's studied *much*
Dis subjict—WERY *much!* *De white folks has,
As well as us, anough o' slavery!*
They would not have us back again as slaves!
And notwithstanding they did not approve
At *fust*, de match 'twixt us and Liberty,
They '*wishes us much joy*'!—THEN LET YER
JOYS ABOUN'!!!"

"I's spoke at instugation, strong,
Of some o' dese old brothrun here, who thought
There were great danger, when de *news* fust come,
Of *mighty pamic! Now* you's quiet, *do
Go long and 'joy yerselves*, jist as ye did

A foe!—I wants de congrugation, *now*,
To sing—and ALL *must* sing—dat good ole hymn
'We's boun' fur de lan', de *happy* lan.' Raise
De hymn, somebody, please, whomever fills
De office of a *Leader in de Choir!*"
No marshalled host did e'er obey command
Of general, more promptly, than did *that*
Vast congregation, yield to wish expressed
By him—who was a JOSHUA, *indeed*,
To *them*—; and the effect was wonderful!

THE EFFECT.

Grief, and Fear, and Consternation,
    Grimly hov'ring o'er that throng,
Started in wild perturbation
    As the joyous *notes* of song,
Led forth by a thousand voices,
    Moved into the airy field,
Like an army that rejoices,
    Confident the foe will yield.
How that airy field then trembled
    'Neath the measured, rapid tread
Of the *chords*, as they assembled
    'Round the TRIO, *conquered*, DEAD!
ECHO sweetly joined the *chorus*,
    Singing in the outer air;
—Or else ANGELS *hovered o'er us*,
    Eager in the joy to share!
Bearing garlands rich, won by her,

Song grew silent, waved her hand,
  To the PLEASURES *standing nigh her*,
    Bidding them the throng command.
Faithfully they did as bidden,
  Wielding wands of magic pow'r,
Till the tardy SUN had hidden,
  From NIGHT's view in TWILIGHT's bow'r,
Night saw Twilight's agitation,
  (Caused by presence of THE SUN,
Who, with such precipitation,
  Had into her bow'r run,)
And, the reason half discerning,
  She, herself, rushed toward the bow'r
—O, *chagrined* was she on learning
  'SUN had GONE *full half an hour!*'
Yet, she gazed with ardent pleasure
  On the radiance which did still
(*Beaming from* the *gems* and *treasures*
  Left by SUN) the bow'r fill.
—Of which radiance* many a nation
  Has the cause to give essayed,
When, since then, through ostentation,
  Twilight has those gems displayed.
Still NIGHT showed of grief signs certain,
  At not gaining partial view
Of the DAY KING, when the curtain
  Of her bow'r proud TWILIGHT drew:
For beneath her "*wraps for summer*,"

---

* Evening after glow.

A PLEASANT REMINISCENCE.   53

   Which she donned, NIGHT held her crown;
And I plainly heard her murmur,
   And as truly, *felt* her frown,
As along the road I speeded,
   Looking for a *transient home;*
While the moments passed unheeded,
   Till to *mansion* I had come.
Murmur after murmur coming,
   I caught, here and there, a word;
Meanings of *all which* by summing,
   I found gist of murmurs heard:
" KING OF DAY, in *all his glory,*
   I once saw on Gibeon,
Where he 'stayed' to see the gory
   Work by ancient Isr'el done,
Till the MOON, my maid of honor,
   Came to vale of Ajalon,
Who had edict laid upon her:
   —'*Halt that Isr'el may slay on!*' "
" I remember well his beauty,
   As he looked upon the plain,
Cheering Isr'el on to duty!
   —*Shall I see him ne'er again?*
Oh! I'd give the brightest jewel
   In my crown (—which is my pride!—)
Could my eyes have brief renewal
   Of that view! *Why* DID *he* HIDE!"

When NIGHT had these murmurs spoken,
   Then her tears began to fall,
5*

Just as if her heart were broken
  —GUSHING—*now;* NOW, *none at all!*
And her sigh did sound like whisper
  Coming from another sphere!
LUNA, hearing, *came and kissed her;*
  —Bade her be of better cheer:
And, at once, NIGHT ceased her weeping;
  Threw her "summer wraps" aside;
Donned her crown, she had been keeping
  'Neath her "*wraps,*" its gems to hide;
And assumed a look quite cheerful,
  So that one would scarce have thought,
She, so lately, had been tearful,
  —Soon I found the '*home*' I sought.

AT A MANSION.

AT A MANSION.

THE WELCOME.

The hospitality proverbial
Of Southern homes, was ne'er more cordial
Than when it welcomed us—*myself* and *steed*—
Supplying each with comforts each did need.
Repast most bountiful was spread for me,
Including many a summer luxury.
Refreshed, I went with host to drawing-room ;
Which was adorned with flowers in bud and bloom,
And paintings hung on snow-white polished wall
—The masterpieces of great artists, *all ;*
(*No,* ONE was wrought by hostess' unskilled brush,
While yet her cheek wore maiden's early blush :
That one my host did o'er the others prize,
Its *faults* appearing *beauties* in *his eyes*—)
And furniture, both modern and antique,
Of which some pieces were of form unique,
Contrived alike for ornament and use

—Some plain, some bearing carvings most profuse.
The tapestry did faithfully display
The grandest scenes in " Mammoth " and " Luray."
In carpet and in rugs were plainly wove
Fierce battle-scenes where Southrons bravely strove
Against great odds and brilliant vict'ries won
(The work of weaving which had all been done
By mother of mine host in private loom.)
It almost seemed that one could hear the boom
And see the smoke burst from the cannon's mouth
—Could see the moving soldiers of both South
And North as promptly they obey command
—See brave men falling pierced on ev'ry hand;
And even *note* the *oozing of the blood*
From half-closed bullet-wound, as tho' one stood
Amid the stirring scenes of actual war:
—The *shuttle* had outstripped the *brush* by far.
The ample fire-place was hid from view
By frame of walnut-wood inlaid with yew,
Containing canvass well-o'erlaid in stitch
With cotton threads of various hues, but which
Was faithfully, yet gorgeously, displayed
A scene to which my soul quite promptly paid
The tribute of appreciative tear,
When clear the *meaning* did to me appear
Of *sentiment beneath*, adroitly told
In characters attractive, wrought in gold:
'Twas just as lifelike as it well could be,
And showed the interview of Grant and Lee
—Beneath it one could at a *distance* see:

*"Within these golden-lettered lines,
A* GEM *of* TRUTH, *half-hidden, shines,*
ABOVE, *in portrait rude, you see*
Two gen'rals SHARING *victory!"*
From golden chandelier there shone a light
Like that of day—so pleasant, yet so bright.
I found that I was not the only guest:
Many were there and ev'ry one expressed
By manner gracious—some by *ardent word*—
Pleasure at meeting me; and when they heard
That I had come but recently from North
In sad ejaculations all burst forth
Almost in concert, speaking words of grief
Profound with ref'rence to the wounded chief,
The conversation ran from theme to theme,
All kindred in their nature, till the stream
Of national events had been surveyed
And all the rocks and shoals which had delayed
The ship of state in outward bound career
Had been identified by landmarks clear
(As laid down in the chart of history)
And located exactly by the free
Employment of "the lead" in trusty hand
Of just, unbiased judgment—and the sand
In *hour-glass* used full quaintly by mine host
Instead of modern time-piece, had almost
Run out the fourth time since I came into
The room. The host reminded us that few
Would be the hours for rest unless we soon
Should to our couches go. " I ask the boon

Louise, of one song first," persuasively
Said one. The lady said evasively;
" I have no *fitting* song. I'm prompt you know
If ready;" " You compose *impromptu*, though,"
Her husband said, for he it was that spoke;
And soon piano felt her skilful stroke;
And her rich voice its melody displayed,
As *words* and *tune impromptu* she essayed.
The husband was a Fed'ral officer
In civil war. Of sev'ral daughters dear
Who *then* graced that same home, Louise was bright
And beautiful as any, who despite
Her long continued efforts to maintain
Her rightful independence, strove in vain
—Like Southland—*to successfully resist*
The will which did on UNION *insist :*
The conflict o'er, a *union* of *love*
Was formed—like that of North and South should
    prove.
Grand was the song Louise, once *rebel-girl*,
(And youngest sister of mine host,) did whirl,
In voice as sweet as that of nightingale
Upon our ears; and far out on the dale
It through the open windows gently flew
And head from wing of many a songster drew
—And *wakeful cottagers from couches, too!*
WE FELT THE THROBBINGS OF THE NATION'S HEART
Whose grief or hope the song in ev'ry part
Expressed, in *meter changed, from time to time,*
—The time becoming *medley,* thus, *sublime.*

The grand achievements of both 'South' and 'North,'
In separate careers, were well set forth
And made the basis of a steadfast hope
That *heart* and *heart* united, both can cope
As one great brotherhood, with ev'ry foe,
Be it invader armed, or home born woe.
Her song the gifted songstress deftly closed
With an address to "*Our Dear Land,*" composed
In words and rhyme which I cannot recall
Yet give the foll'wing as *a hint*—that's all :
" Thou *Freedom's* great *Temple* art set on a hill !
The sheen of thy splendors doth all the earth fill
When cloudless the *sun* of *prosperity* falls
On thy jewel-crowned spires and gold-covered walls
And when the dark *night of adversity* throws
Its deep shades about thee, thine altar then glows
With *fire from heaven* (SELF-SACRIFICE.)   All
Thine inner component parts—Gold carvèd WALL,
(*Pure Wisdom* with *Practical Knowledge well graced;*)
Thy MOSAIC FLOOR, (*Truth* with *Justice inlaced;*)
Thy CANOPY, (*Hope, with a pure Faith inwrought ;*)
VESSELS OF SERVICE, (*Institutions, blood-bought;*)
—*These all with inherent bright radiance shine,*
Which joins with the light that doth beam from thy shrine,
And streams through thy windows and quickly illumes
The mount where thou standest—*the darkness consumes!* "
When song was finished—after proper word

Of praise, (well-earned,) from most of us who heard—
We, at request of host, in worship bowed,
While he as priest spoke praise and prayer aloud.
Some moments passed: Louise's husband rose
And said: "I thank you heartily, for those
Warm sentiments that you have just expressed
For '*Union of the States*,' which in MY BREAST
Holds higher place than even my own life!
—That *song* has made you to me *dearer*, wife,
Than ever: and I hope 'twill not amiss
Be reckoned that I now imprint a kiss
Upon the lips which uttered those sweet words."
She, blushing, said; "Your conduct well affords
Example of the *slowness* on the part
Of *Northern mind* to *read the Southern heart!*
Full oft have I expressed such sentiment
As words of that *new song* did represent!
So has the South, through many years, by deed
Expressed her love for Union; yet the meed
Of just acknowledgment has been denied
Till now, by '*North*,' who has the '*South*' decried!
The 'North's' complaints, most bitter, plainly prove
That 'North' thinks 'South' *has reason* NOT *to
love!*
O that the bond between the States might be
Like bond uniting hearts of—*you* and *me!!*
This last she spoke *adroitly*, as with smile
She rose and stood beside her husband; while
The company applauded with a *shout*
In miniature, and *rose*, *too*, to pass out

At bidding of the HOST : *"Let's seek repose*
Before old ' DIXIE' for the day-dawn crows !"
Just as we moved to go, through open door
An aged man came slowly in. Before
The company whose hearts were struck with fear
He stood awhile in silence. We could hear
The beating of our hearts while old man spoke
In accents which, *on host's ear* ONLY broke
The silence deep, to others marred alone
By frightened host's quick heart-throbs, *and their
 own:*
" Be not alarmed for I have only come
In kindness. I have oft within this home
Of ardent patriotism in the days
Of years long gone in various ways
Been entertained with marked esteem by those
Who then the happy household did compose.
Where are they now ? Gone into spirit-land !
Here, they were pious—there a sainted band !
Direct descendant of such noble race
Could not refuse *a stranger,* e'en, a place
Within the circle fraught with friendship's charm !
—*I smiled on thee,* a BABE, *John !* Fear no harm !"
The host received surprise in heavy stroke
When thus he heard his name by old man spoke.
Speechless and pale he tottered to a chair
—Speechless indeed were all, till *I* said ; " Where
You may elect shall be your seat, my friend :
And speech is free ! Speak till you choose to end !"
I glanced t'ward hostess : *pallid too she* was,

Yet bowed approval of my *coup de grace*.
While, by degrees, the company grew calm,
Seated, the old man stroked his beard with palm
And speech resumed, in *voice* which did not break
The outer silence and which, yet, did make
Impressions on our minds as strong and clear
As *common* voices do which sound in air.
The officer, who saw the old man, gazed
Alternately at him and us, amazed
That we should listen as tho' human word
Were spoke by stranger—*for no voice* HE *heard*,
We listened, rapt: "Attracted by that song
Whose melody was greeted, all along
The highways and the by-paths, and within
The homes, by those who heard it, with a din
Of praise, I came to give your hearts relief
From deep suspense about the wounded *chief;*
And, also, timely comfort to extend
Concerning dangers which you fear impend
Above your much-loved, mourning land's career,
And which in future, both remote and near,
May fall, producing havoc with its peace
And welfare, till that havoc find surcease
In ruin."

"*Just* as one on mountain's side
Can see large objects floating on a tide
Whose waters broad and deep do sweep amain
By mountain's base and through the neighb'ring
    plain,
So view I facts which did in past transpire :

And, as one standing on a point much higher
—Say *top*—can see the streamlets as they come
Away, each from its isolated home
—*Now* hiding as it makes its pathway through
A forest thick ; *now* coming into view
Where verdant meadow and grain-growing land
Express their greeting as on either hand
They smile; *now* lavishing on boggy fen
Its gifts; delighting, *now*, the rocky glen
With music and with dancing, as along
It hastens joyously to join the throng
Of waters as they mingle in a grand
Procession *to the gates at ocean's strand,*
Through which have passed the waters gone before
To realm so wondrous, they came back no more,
So view I from the eminence I hold
In life's great mount, events yet to be *told*
As '*having come,*' by promptly speaking *Time,*
The *Usher.*"
　　　　　　" I can see result of crime
Committed by Guiteau to be *the death*
Of Garfield, (notwithstanding ev'ry breath
The nation breathes the meanwhile be a prayer;)
But not those evils which would bring despair
To patriot-hearts—which you have seemed to fear—
Referred to in the song which still I hear
In plaintive echo ringing through the cells
Where *Mem'ry,* like a prince close-cloistered, dwells."
" See! Arthur rules! and when he leaves the chair
The nation's righteous judgment ev'rywhere

Express warm approval of the course
Of his administration. None the worse
Career does that of his successor prove;
For government whilst *he* holds helm doth move,
Like steamship on the deep, despite the wind
And currents which oppose—its course confined
Successfully to line resolved upon
When preparations for the voyage begun.
His rule will universal joy afford,
For *union* will in spirit be restored
Ere that 'successor' leave the chair of state."
—"The *parties* of the land will alternate
In holding the control of government
For periods of irregular extent
The *party-spirit* which has done such harm
Will be subdued and cease to cause alarm.
Prosperity will be compelled to store
Much surplus fruit of labor, and explore
New fields wherein the growing family
Of *Enterprise* may, without trammel, be
Employed. The country's *commerce* will extend:
The nations north and south, with it will blend
And form 'THE CLOSE COMMERCIAL UNION
OF BOTH AMERICAS—IN INT'RESTS ONE.' "
—" The various, *vast*, resources of the *South*
Will then developed be; and ev'ry mouth
Will wonder speak at the abundant yield
Of wealth by forest, mountain, stream and field,
In timber, gold and coal, in fish and grain:
And '*South*' will rise and occupy again

The place once held by her—'*before the war;*'
And win the name of '*Great*,' both near and far.
Then honor will accorded be to those
Who did in days of civil-war compose
The '*People of The South;*' who, being true
To their convictions, bravely, nobly threw
Their treasures, pleasures, comforts, lives—*their
    all!*—
On altars of those States which they did call
Respectively their own; and durst engage
To hold by war, their rights as priceless wage.
Then, *too,* will *North* and *East* and *West* be proud
Of record made '*in arms*' by what in loud
Reproachful tones they now delight to name
As 'REBEL ARMY'—*just as now* LEE'S *fame
Surpasses* GRANT'S *in all the foreign lands,*
While STONEWALL JACKSON'S, *to* NONE *second
    stands!*
Then will Caucasians in the Southern-land
Regard the *loss* of '*Southern Cause,*' as *grand
Misfortune* and *Good-fortune intertwined.*
*Mis*fortune, in that *rights* which all mankind
Hold dear, *by pow'r were rudely trodden down:*
*Good-*fortune, in that where those rights were thrown
In lifeless form, lo! presently there grew
Luxuriant benefits in form of new
Prosperity, whose blooms and fruit gave joy
Throughout the land whose rights *Pow'r* did destroy!"
—" These things successive, like the ocean-waves,

I see approaching ; and my spirit craves
Their presence, *all at once ;* but we must wait—
If some come early, others must come late !
Yet, in their coming, now they seem to rush
With eager haste, that they may put to blush
Each of the ages which the world has known
—*E'en that* which men have named the *golden* one."
" Some troubles, true, will meanwhile fall to lot
Of this great land, which I have mentioned not :
But they the gen'ral peacefulness will mar,
Like clouds, (as small as that one seen afar
By prophet seemed to be to his keen eye,)
Would, by their shadows, should they swiftly fly
Across the sun, a transient darkness throw
Upon a gorgeous landscape all aglow
As though 'twere overlaid with burnished gold
—Like scenes which Fairies showed in days of old !"
" I hope these *future* facts, foretold by me,
Will, all your minds, from dark forebodings free.
The present *gloom* which hangs o'er ev'ry part
Of this great land, will, not long hence, depart.
—When *Garfield dies,* as *shroud* the *nation's gloom*
Will, with his lifeless form, *be laid in tomb :*
Though *sadness* will on ev'ry heart be left,
For ev'ry heart will feel itself bereft."
He stood upon his feet, as if to go ;
Then settled back into his chair—so slow
The motion, that we scarce perceived him move—
Meanwhile he gazed intent as tho' he strove
To view some distant scene hard to discern ;

Pale, now; and, NOW, *his cheeks did* fairly *burn.*
Then Satisfaction with her wand illumed
His countenance, and he his speech resumed :
"A scene, till late, by me quite unobserved,
Has just received attention it deserved
As it developed rapidly before
My view; at which I wondered all the more
Because, though I had seen the like, quite *strange*
It seemed. First came a *life,* which soon did change
To *death,* the mute and down-cast harbinger
Of *new-born life,* a bright-faced messenger
Whose cheerful look full plainly gift foretold
As coming soon (—*which it in hand did hold!*—)
For one who, toiling, had, in other day,
To gain that life giv'n other life away!
A beauteous cotton-bloom arrayed in white,
At *morn* stepped forth to greet a stranger's sight:
At *noon* he looked, and lo! its *robe was new,*
Or else had *changed from white* to *pink* in hue :
Expectant of new change, at *eventide*
He looked again for bloom. Lo! *it had died!*
And on the ground it lay—*its robes a shroud,*
In color pretty as a purple cloud
On which the setting sun has thrown, askance,
The radiance of benignant farewell glance!
The stranger sighed; and, might have shed a tear,
Had not the *owner* of the plant drawn near
And *touched the* POD, *which stranger had not seen,*
Arrayed in lustrous garb of royal green.
That touch had force of '*magic*', for the '*bowl*'

Or pod, its outer wrappings did unroll,
And to the *planter* held, *in open hand*
A *snow-white jewel prized in ev'ry land!*"
"Should not the *lesson* taught, our *thoughts command*
Amid the rapid changes in our land?
Ah! yes! Tho' pretty *blooms of prospect* change
And pass away, too soon, beyond the range
Of our fond view, we may expect to find
Some *much-prized good*, which lay concealed behind
The prospect that engrossed admiring view
—*The real* FRUIT *from which the* BLOSSOM GREW!
—A *good, as unlike prospect, passed away,*
As '*bowl*' was unlike '*bloom,*' which prostrate lay!"
—His voice was silent; and his chair
Was empty! *When* he went or *where*
None knew. All were amazed. The *host*,
Almost in whisper, said: "The ghost
Of him who on my infant head
Baptismal waters poured, now dead
For many, *many* years, was he
Who came and went mysteriously.
Full oft when in the flesh he came
To visit us; and met the same
Glad welcome that a kinsman would
Desire, from all. He was as good
As mortal man e'er gets to be
In this estate; and all that he
Has shown us in prophetic view,
May be relied upon as true!"
These words had scarce been spoke when lo! again

The *old man* stood in view, distinct as when
He first came in; and said in same *strange kind*
Of *voice*, which made *impressions on the mind*
Yet did not sound upon the ear: " I came,
And one, yea *but* one *stranger saw!* My name
By all, *except that one*, should have been known :
My words should my identity have shown !
I *go* a *friend*, (oft seen,) *unknown* by *those
With whom I've been, for years, in joys and woes!*
I have lived long: yet, oh! the cheering truth,
In my old age, I have renewed my youth!
My youthful vigor, too, shall grow apace
While in the South dwells the *Caucasian* race !"

  Whilst silently we gazed
   On apparition strange,
  Than ever more amazed
   We grew at seeing change,
  (As if by magic) wrought
   In form and feature, too,
  Of what we all had thought
   An aged man. A new
  And wond'rous vision stood
   Before us. *Age* and *youth*,
  In ev'ry way they *could*
   Be blended, were, forsooth,
  In countenance, which shone
   With light that *grew* apace
  —First star-like, then like moon
   At full.—The form changed place

And passed out open door.
  We followed, then it rose
And spread in size, *till o'er*
  The South, as maiden throws
Her wrappings loosely on,
  Its drapery of light
It threw: while closely drawn
  Near brow, though it was night,
A rain-bow crowned a smile
  Which greeted us and all
Who *upward* looked: for, while
  We looked, words seemed to fall
Which we did understand:
  Immortal HOPE IN GOD
Is PATRON *of Southland*;
  And greeting sends abroad."

THE EXPLANATION.

The " officer," a man
  Of learning and of " wit,"
When silence came, began
  An explanation fit
Of what we saw and heard:
  "The *vision* which you view,
And *sounds* that seem like word
  Addressed from air to you,
Are mysteries profound,
  Indeed. But *wond'rous things*,
In nature's realm, *abound:*

Yet science oft-times brings
Relief to some extent
—The *mystery* explains
—Dispels *bewilderment;*
Tho' *wonder* still remains.
"Imagination, pressed
To act by one in fear,
Will to that one distressed,
Make horrid things appear,
Another, nigh scans forms
He has strong wish to see:
For Fancy, sly, transforms
Anything—*bush* or *tree!*
Oft-times one hears his name
Spoken in place quite lone;
Yet cannot tell whence came
The sound—and sees no one.
Mirage on desert seen
By travelers alert
For some oasis green,
Deceives, oft, those *expert.*
Mirage seen out at sea,
When ships appear in air,
From sailors *old* drives *glee*
—In *fear* makes *young* ones stare."
"Explained, each wonder proves
Effect of hidden cause
—As pivot-magnet moves
By one of nature's laws."
"This *scene* (to say I dare)

Is but *mirage—The* THOUGHT
And HOPE of SOUTH, *on air*
In wond'rous image wrought
The *scene*, indeed, *is real*
—The *focus* at which meet
The *burning hopes for weal,*
With which 'South' seems replete.
But, *voice* was your hearts' fruit,
Imagination made
Articulate to suit
The scene above displayed."

———

Long gazed we at the scene, till spoke
Our host; whose words thus gently broke
The thread of solemn thought: " 'Tis night
As yet; let's seek the couch, lest light
Of day should, haply, us surprise
Ere waiting slumber close our eyes."

THE ECHOING SHELL.

When host had *"lighted me to bed,"* and left
Me with: *"Good-night!"* I was as one bereft
—So very sad and lonely did I feel.
I sighed; and wondered why a cloud should steal
—So dark!—between me and my wonted cheer;
And strove to fan it off by rudeness, sheer,
Of stroke with gleeful thought: but all in vain—
The cloud would yield to stroke; then come again—

I forced attention to the things I found
Of interest to a stranger, all around
The room. I read: "*Rare shells from distant sea,
Each labeled—some from nearer waters—free
For ev'ry stranger-guest* to look upon,
And choose one as his own." I took up one;
And, closing rosewood box in which they lay,
And sighing yet again, I turned away
And sought my waiting couch—delightful bed!—
And placed the "chosen shell" beneath my head.
Soon I was lost in sleep; and pleasant dreams,
Clothed in gay colors like the sun's last beams,
Attended me: and, yet, occasional sigh
Did faintly whisper through the dreamland-sky.
My dreams conducted me throughout South-land:
The sigh, (I found,) was whir of sword in hand
Of *Death*, presaging grief to nation, deep;
At which my eyes shed burning tears in sleep.
I woke and rose, while dawn had not yet come.
A strange yet sweet-voiced murmur filled the room.
Articulate it was not; still, it seemed,
At times, like voices heard whilst yet I dreamed.
Again I sought my couch: the murmur thrilled
Me with amazement painful; for it filled
My ear—the one which next the pillow lay—
With *words* consecutive! I brushed away
The cold sweat sprinkled on my brow by *Fear;*
And wished my ears had not the pow'r to hear
Till day should dawn. But *Mem'ry* broke the spell
Of Fear by pointing with her wand to shell,

Which I had taken from the box it graced,
And, thoughtless underneath my pillow placed.
Fear fled; and smiling *Wonder* gently came,
And soothed my spirit into pleasant frame,
When I the tiny shell placed to my ear,
In order well its whisperings to hear.
Its voice was but *an echo*, in which rang
The sentiments of thousands, who *there* sang
In *chorus*—as the Nereïds of the sea,
Blend all their songs in murmur on the lee.
Those sentiments I plainly did detect,
In murmurs of the shell, to be *respect*
And *admiration* true for *some great chief*,
Whose *state* was object of high *pride*, not grief,
To Southrons, all. At first I could not tell
Who that chief was; but, list'ning long and well,
I heard his name, distinctly, oft-times spoke
—*Each voice, each time*, a blessing did invoke
" On him who represents 'The Cause now Lost'
—The Cause whose justice is the Southron's boast."

I rose and looked abroad; and saw that *Night*
Was driving swiftly down the eastern height;
While, holding lamp at chariot-front, *Moon* lent
Her aid against the chance of accident;
And *thought* I saw, faint gleaming, far away,
The radiant smile of eager, waiting, *Day*,
—Who, while he rests, entrusts to Night's command
The steeds which *Time* gave *both* to hold in hand.

I made my toilet; then the "label" viewed
Upon the "chosen shell;" and then pursued
The plan prescribed, thus: "*Stranger-guests who take
Shells from this rosewood box as theirs, must make
Full entry of their names and homes; and well
Describe, on tablet* HERE, *each chosen* shell."
All this I did—I gave my name and home,
Described my shell and told whence it had come.

The "*label*," with most wondrous art, had been
Indited so that naught but *dots* were seen
When looked at as a whole; but as each word
Was closely viewed, *it magnified,* appeared!
I read it till on memory it remained,
—These are the words, in full, which it contained:
"This shell of wondrous *echo,* came
From near the home of one whom *Fame*
Enrolled, while young, among the *great,*
—The brave and wise—in field and state:
And when rude force, that *flag* destroyed
Whose honor all his pow'rs employed,
Fame, for his brow, (of *friends'* warm love
And foes' abuse close interwove,)
Prepared a *special,* BRILLIANT *crown,*
Which marks a *glory all his own;*
While Fortune gave him splendid home
Where southern Gulf's bright waters foam
In gentle waves on its north shore;
And mingling with their pæan-roar,
The Southrons' whispered blessings greet

The Hero—*greatest in defeat!*
— *Would you those whispered blessings hear,*
In ECHO? *Place this shell to ear!*
Taking this gift, say *this*—no more:
'*Honor to Hero at Beauvoir!*'"

Reflection, short, led me to think it best
To leave the shell for ev'ry "*stranger-guest*"
To see and *hear*, at any future day
—I marked it : " *Chos'n but not yet tak'n away!*"
—Perhaps you ask : " Did you *condition* meet
Of taking wondrous echo-shell, and *greet*
In word the " Hero at Beauvoir?'" Ah! Well;
This I will *say : I did not take the shell!*

DAY-DAWN.

Like healthful babe from pleasant dreaming,
The *morning* woke with face all beaming
And sent her smile o'er nature streaming
Which sat the world and heav'ns a-gleaming;
While earth and air with joy were teeming.
On ev'ry hand the fowl were winging;
On flexile boughs the squirrels were swinging;
And to the teat glad young were clinging,
While voices manifold were ringing
In human song or conversation
And dumb brute's rude communication
Of neighborly congratulation
To others on participation

Of prospects thrown from hand of *Day-Light*
Whose coming brought those brutes glad respite
From loneliness they felt at midnight,
And restlessness at morning twilight.
It seemed that *Morn* with hand was waving
To all whose opened eyes were craving
Beauteous scenes of Nature's graving;
Or whose desires, fierce grown, were raving
For food or draught or pleasant laving
To come forth from their place of resting
And gratify each wish thus testing
The skill of Nature in investing
Her works with pow'r to yield high pleasure
Without alloy and in full measure;
From whose abundant varied treasure
They *all* might take at will and leisure.
  "How bright a day!"
  (—I could but say,
 As in the lawn of host I stood
 And gazed at glorious field and wood—)
  "How glad should we
  At all times be
That in a world so full of joy
We live—where we find sweet employ
  For taste and touch;
  And just as much
To gratify the eye and ear,
Through ev'ry season of the year!"
  Then Memory,
  With step most free,

Rushed swiftly back to days of yore,
Conveying me midst scenes once more
  In which I moved
  With those I loved
When Youth and I companions were
—And Joy also, for Woe's hot tear
  Had, then, not yet
  My young cheek wet.—
And as those scenes passed in review,
"This world's the home of *Joy*, 'tis true;"
  I said; "but oh!
  Who does not know
That in this world dark *Sorrow, too*,
Makes her abode the whole year through:
  And even while
  Joy's thrilling smile
New life to human spirit lends,
The shadow of *her* form she sends,
  Producing night
  In midst of light,
And, all unseen, wounds with her dart
The unsuspecting gleeful heart!"
  While thus I stood
  In thoughtful mood
I felt the gentle touch of hand;
And saw a child beside me stand,
  Who met my gaze
  With bland amaze,
Yet said: "I've come to call you home
To breakfast, sir; papa says, 'come'!"

And as we walked
Slowly, we talked,
I found him wise for one so young;
—Possessor, too, of *gifted tongue!*
"I'm sad," he said,
"For Garfield's dead!
His *deeds as President* were few,
And yet a *brilliant hope* they threw
On future days,
(Grandmother says,)
That blessings might come to Southland,
Conducted by his faithful hand;
And well revealed
What *wrongs* concealed
—*The eagerness of* SOUTHERN *mind*
To honor NORTHERN *actions kind* :—
Much as, at night,
The brilliant light
At locomotive's front doth send
The promise of a coming friend,
And plain reveals
What *night* conceals
—*The friends who at the station stand*
With welcome in both eye and hand."
Less fast I stepped
—Then *stopped*, and *wept*
As that dear boy in touching strain
Spoke of the " *kindred of the slain* "
—How they must be
In agony

At death of one to them so dear;
—How that this world would sad appear
    To them for aye
    (Till their death-day)
Tho' ev'rything should wear a smile
And strive their sorrow to beguile.
    " But oh! " said he,
    " Bereft are we
Both old and young throughout Southland
By act of that vile murd'rer's hand! "
    His *eye flashed fire!*
    His *voice rose high'r!*
He seemed to be most strangely changed,
As in high eloquence he ranged
    Beyond the reach
    Of my poor speech
Here to relate what then he said
(While *Mercury's* wings waved o'er his head,)
    Portraying grief
    Without relief
Which had like *dark*-winged angel come
Afflicting ev'ry Southern home
    —As in the yore
    An angel bore
Death on his wings, who slew *first-born*
And made Egyptian homes forlorn.
    Attempt I made
    —*Again* essayed—
To break his spell of grief profound,
By telling him that *Garfield's wound*

Might yet be healed
To skill might yield—
That hope had not entirely fled;
The President was not yet dead:
But *thought* well-meant
In vain was spent
—My tongue cleaved to my roof each time,
While he continued *speech sublime!*
Long tarried we
Beneath a tree
Whose leafful boughs protection gave
From morning-sun's broad shimmering wave.
When we reached "home,"
Tears still would come;
For o'er my soul *emotion rolled,*
Caused by his thought and language bold
(*—I feel it yet!*
—My eye is wet!—)
As, on the ocean, billows rise
And throw their spray in *Neptune's* eyes,
Long after blast
Has landward passed,
And gone to rest in mountain-cave
—Its *force still ling'ring on the wave.*
When noon had come
The child from home
On errand went; and I made bold
In faithful word to well unfold
To family
The cause why we

Had our return as long delayed,
And underneath the beech-tree staid.
　They list'ned well;
　And I could tell
Their deep emotion by their look,
As though I read in printed book.
　When I had done,
　The *sire* begun:
"Our child * has pow'r of thought and word
But to *repeat* what he has heard,
　Oft with a gush
　His words will rush:
He seems to *speak extempore*,
While he *recites from memory*.
　The gesture, too,
　And accent, *true*
Or *false*, he sees or hears one use,
He faithfully will reproduce.
　Mother and he
　Sweetly agree:
Oft he repeats her words and ways
And sometimes adds, ' *Grandmother says*,'
　Whate'er to-day
　You've heard him say
About the suff'ring President

---

* The prototype of the "child" was *Charlie Shannon*, a *prodigy in memory*, who could repeat *long speeches* after hearing them read *once* (or *twice* at most.) He was on exhibition at the age of seven years, in Baltimore and elsewhere in this country, and went to Europe.

Was fruit of hours with mother spent,
    Since we first heard
    The *stunning* word
On yesterday, ere yet the sun
His upward course had half-way run."
    Thus spoke the sire.
    His eye *flashed* fire!
And rising grandly to his feet
He eloquently did repeat
    Like thought and *word*
    With those which stirred
My soul, when dumb, in weeping mood,
Before the child, on lawn, I stood.
    He then showed *scar*
    Received in war
Upon his cheek; and sev'ral more,
He said, he on his person wore
    With honest pride
    That he had vied
With soldiers brave in doing most
For Southern cause now long since lost:
    "Because we fought
    For what we thought,
And *still think* 'CAUSE OF LIBERTY'
—'*The Right of each State to be Free*'—
    And on the field
    We strove to shield
Our *land* from *desolation's tread,*
Our *homes* from *desecration, dread!*
    But war is o'er;"

(Said he,) "*ne'er more*
May its fell spirit sway the hand
Of those who dwell within our land!"
"Much should we love
Who still do move
Along the path of earthly life,
Survivors of that deadly strife!
In *vain*, indeed,
Did myriads bleed
And die on war's embattled plain,
Where *brothers* died by *brothers slain*,
If in this land
All do not stand,
As *brethren*, in that bond of love
To *break* which WAR *too weak* did prove!"
"The deed late done
At Washington
Must have been act of *only two*
—A *man*, exposed to human view,
And *fiend*, unseen,
(Behind the screen)—
These two alone, performed the deed
That makes the nation's heart now bleed.
And could *this hand*
My wish command,
Upon them both, *unseen* and *seen*,
Their pangs should be tenfold more keen
Than ever came
In *eager flame*
To torture writhing human flesh,

Or woke in *hades,* shrieks afresh!"
"Oh! May God shield
Our *Chief,* Garfield,
From death, however deep may be
The wound that gives him agony!
As *soldier,* true,
He wore the '*blue*';
But, tho' he fought against our rights,
He *bravely* bore him through those fights
Where his lot fell;
For which he *well*
Deserves, in common with the brave
Of ev'ry land what *soldiers* crave
—'*Best boon of fame*
—A *brave* man's *name*—
The epithet of *Hero*': and
Throughout our wide-extended land
Both *North* and *South*
Should ev'ry mouth
Speak *kindly* of the President
Of these great States in Union blent,
—A *union* SURE
NOW TO ENDURE,
Since '*Sov'reign Right of State to Break
From Union*', which was put at stake
In war, *was lost,*
(—At what great *cost*
In *violence to justice,* and
In human blood which drenched the land,
It *matters not!*

Be that forgot!)
THE UNION CHERISHED NOW BY ALL
WITHIN THE STATES CAN NEVER FALL!"
    Yet of the TRUE
    And TRIED MEN, *few*
Within the *South*, do now profess
Repentance, saying '*We confess*
    We were unwise
    To sacrifice
The benefits of union
With ALL *the States, for few or none*
    We should have gained
    Had we maintained
Successfully, '*that* STATE MUST *be*
An INDEPENDENT SOV'REIGNTY'
    —A principle
    Which never will
Be made untenable by *force*
Of *truth :* by *force of arms*, of course,
    It may be crushed,
    As has been hushed
The *voice* of *many* a *living truth*,
Too *harsh* for Pow'r's ear, forsooth!"
    "For *tho'* we see
    These States *should* be,
    In *these* days, joined in union strong,
(E'en if to each there should belong
    The *right* as '*State*'
    To *separate*
—As 'SOV'REIGNTY' *alone to stand ;*

Regarded such on ev'ry hand,)
Because the *best*,
True *interest*
Of all concerned depends upon
The maintenance of Union,
Still we maintain,
That all our slain,
And soldiers who survived the war,
Unhurt or wearing battle-scar,
Achieved a fame
Well worth the name;
That cause was ne'er, on earth, more just
Than ours; *that what* the North did thrust
On us, we took
Because forsook
Us at that hour both strength and hope
—We could not with foe, *longer cope!*
Strange would it be
If we should see
A good in *ruin* which befell
The South—a ruin which might well
Be styled *complete*,
Bringing defeat
Of armies;. razing to the ground
Our social fabric; building mound
Of the débris
Beneath which, we,
Caucasians of the South, were doomed
To lie, *alive*, and, yet, *entombed*,
—From which we rose

By mighty throes
Only to find we must rebuild
Our fabric as our late foes willed;
    Who, while they fought
    Us, only sought,
They said, the Union to maintain,
Yet, having chance, could not refrain
    (Deceitful foes!)
    From aiming blows
At *institution* we did prize,
And which they viewed *with envious eyes!*"
    " We think it wise
    To utilize
The opportunities which lie
Before us—faithfully to try
    T' obey as best
    We can, behest
Of duty as she speaks each hour,
While we regret we had not pow'r
    To win in war
    What we strove for!
As one into whose cherished home
A murderer has boldly come
    —Killed great and small,
    Wife, children, all—
His vacant home does cherish still,
Bowing to Heav'n's permissive will,
    While at same time
    He does no crime
By wish that to his cherished home

The fiendish murd'rer had not come,
  Or that his strength
  Of arm, at length,
Had proved enough to break the arm
Of murd'rer ere it wrought such harm."
" We do not cast
  Upon our past
The shadow of reproachful look
Because our rights we undertook
  (—Rights dear as life
  And worth the strife
We strove—) to gain ; tho' rights once gained
Might have cost much to be maintained.
  But we do strive
  From us to drive
All feelings of resentment, just
Howe'er they be, t'ward those who thrust
  Upon us wrong,
  And with a strong
And fiercely vengeful, war-clad arm,
Strove to lay on us ev'ry harm.
  Being compelled
  By war to yield
To *will,* and *share the lot* of those
Who did *repulsive bond* impose,
  Like maids of yore
  Whom Romans bore
Away as wives from Sabine homes,
We feel that *union-bond* becomes
  Less bad each day :

Tho' still, as *they*
Did, so do we sincerely *deem*
Relations past worth high esteem!
Of our *past* proud,
We speak aloud
So that the world may hear our praise
Of those brave men whom God did raise
As leaders, great
In '*field*' and '*state*;'
Who consecrated all their skill
To carry'ng out the people's will
To have a free
Confed'racy
Of Southern States, (in *int'rest one*,)
United by *will*-bond alone.
And the result
Of each insult
Shot t'ward them like a venomed dart
Is but to make each *Southern* heart
Hold in contempt
Those, whose attempt
Thus to malign the South's great men
Is *mean* and *cowardly:* [as when,
Coming round
A captive bound
—A chief o'ercome by numbers great—
Low dastard savages, elate
At chance to show
Their skill with bow
At human target without fear

Of hurt (*yet fearing* to *go near*)
    Do shoot and wound,
    Then look around
That they safe exit-way may choose,
Should chieftain's thongs by chance come loose :]
    So, Sabine maid
    Who homage paid
As wife to Roman would have burned
With anger—would away have turned
    Contemptu'sly
    From him, if he
Had stigmatized her kindred dear,
Thus offering *insult* to her.
    Yet just as she
    Did, thus do we
—*Hold with firm grasp of ardent love*
RELATIONS NEW, which we approve!
    True, now and then,
    It may be, when
Before Injustice' blow we reel,
Our hearts back to *far past* will steal,
    And seek relief
    From present grief
By living o'er again, in *thought*,
Days which to us with joys were fraught :
    But soon they come
    —*Our hearts*—back home,
While *thought*, returning *passes by*
The '*day* of *struggle*,' with *clos'd eye*."
    " We, Southrons, feel

That pointed steel
Could not have giv'n our hearts more pain
Than did the news: '*Garfield is slain!*';
For he belongs
To us: *his wrongs*
Are *ours:* we love him; and, if need
There were, *our hearts for him would bleed!*"
"O sad the day
When we survey
The evils which have fall'n on
Our land of late—and in years gone!
Yet ancient Job,
(—Whom foes did rob)
When various agencies employed
By Satan, ruthlessly destroyed
His gathered wealth,
His cherished health,
His servants, children; from him turned
His consort's heart, which should have burned
T'ward him with love,
Said: '*He above*
The skies, did all those blessings give
And take away; HE *shall receive*
My praise!'—Thus *we*
Should strive to be
Content; since *we, too,* recognize
A HEAVENLY RULER, *good* and *wise*,
Who oft allows
What reason shows
To be result by evil wrought;

And yet, the suff"rers oft are brought
    To see glad days
    When he displays
His pow'r and goodness with free hand;
And *joys*, hearts *lately sad*, command!"
" This land of ours,
    Where evil pow'rs
Crossed brothers' arms in deadly strife
—Made havoc of all joys of life—
    Through weary years,
    Which wrote with tears
And *blood* their records, fadeless as
The color which the cypress has—
    This land whose brow
    Does even now
Wear shadow of a heart-felt woe
Because its wounded chief lies low,
    May from that Hand
    Which doth command
The universe, such gifts receive
That, *o'er the past 'twill cease to grieve!*"
    Thus spoke a man
    In whose veins ran
True Southern blood; and in whose mind
" The Lost Cause " once had been enshrined.
I travelled thence from place to place
Through town and country. Ev'ry face
I met, wore sign of settled gloom
'Midst which no ray of joy did loom.
Men field-work left, and rapid strode

To intercept me on the road;
Children in cottage-yard cried: "*Wait!*"
And came with mother to the gate;
Mechanics stood in work-shop doors;
Apprentices stopped doing chores;
The doctor driving fleet-foot horse,
Abruptly checked his rapid course;
Pupils of school, in solemn mood,
At school-house door and windows stood,
While teacher, hatless, book in hand,
At road-side, 'neath a tree, did stand;
Sellers and buyers, at the stores,
Crowded the porches and the doors,
At my approach—*all full intent*
To learn how was "The President."

THE RETURN.

THE RETURN.

SUN-SET SCENE.

Returning northward t'ward my home,
When many a mile alone I'd come
O'er level-land and hill and stream,
Thro' forest shade and warm sun-beam,
Where nature spread before my view
(Arrayed in dress of varied hue,)
Her works of skill, in kind and shape
Of leaf and flow'r and broad landscape
Most wonderful, I stopped, for rest
Of self and steed, upon the crest
Of hill, which rose high over plain;
And Southward turned my eyes again.
From throne, in West, of mountain peaks,
O'erlaid with ash-hued pearl, with streaks
Of emerald, and richly lined
With snow-white satin cloud combined
With amber strip and azure fold
Looped up with sprays of purest gold,

Beneath ethereal canopy,
The Sun, in royal panoply,
Threw golden gems with sapphires fraught,
Which field and flood and forest caught
With eager hands, as do the poor
Take gifts, and smiled and asked for more.
" Stay long, O gen'rous Prince ", I cried,
"And pour thy gifts in constant tide
On Southland ! Let thy smile illume,
If possible, her people's gloom ! "

A Voice Against the South.

When I said that, a faint voice came
And spoke to me, but gave no name :
" The Southern States compose a land
In which there dwells a teeming band
Of men, than whom you cannot find
More false and vile among mankind !
Against their country they rebelled,
And loud and long for freedom yelled ;
While they themselves, in bondage held
Their fellow-men, (by rod compelled
To do hard toil as life-long slaves
To masters, who at heart were knaves,
Denied those gifts which nature craves
—Good food and raiment,—till their graves
Were entered gladly, as the waves
Glad rush to beach, to hide from storm
Which whips their dripping, trembling form,

Pursues them even to the shore,
And smites till they are seen no more :)
Then, having long and fiercely fought
Against their country's flag for naught,
Except for privilege full fraught
With ill to all—e'en them who sought
That privilege—and, having been
Compelled to cease their war of sin
By force of skilful arms, with grin,
(Discerned full well beneath the thin
Transparent veiling which they wore,
As mourners for the part they bore,
In drenching this fair land with gore,)
They asked to be received once more
Beneath the flappings of that flag
Which to the dust they strove to drag;
And promised they would never lag
Behind the foremost who might brag
How swift he'd run at each behest
Of duty to the *Union* blest!
They were received; and, yet, they stood
Compacted close—a brotherhood
Of traitors foul—in wistful mood
Awaiting chance again to flood
This land with trouble's darksome tide
On which both they and sons might ride,
With sails before the blast spread wide,
As pirates civic, and provide
Themselves, by force, with what belongs
To others 'mid the noble throngs

Of men who crushed rebellion's wrongs
And sang, at last, proud vict'ry's songs
—Which *still the trembling air prolongs!*
And just as eagle watches lamb,
Which once his talons held, till dam
And shepherd drove him from the field,
Which he reluctantly did yield,
So do those men watch Afric's race,
(Whom they once held in firm embrace,
With fondest love, but to devour
And feed upon, and, thus get pow'r
To rise to heights they had not gained,)
Now, that compelled, they have refrained
From using beaks and talons, too;
While on their eyries, close in view,
They shake their feathers, and on high
Lift wings which they would gladly try
In flight t'ward prey so lately theirs;
—Which now, though wounded, safety shares
Beneath the watchful eye and hand
Of chiefest shepherd of the land."

Whence came the voice, I could not tell.
No form could I discern, tho' well
I all my pow'rs of vision tried,
And searched the air both far and wide.
But while I searched, a second voice
(Whose accents, sweet, made me rejoice,)
Addressed me; and a form, most clear
Did just in front of me appear,

—A female, fair, whose robe was girt
With zone of stars; the flowing skirt
With rainbow hues, all intertwined,
Was rich adorned; and close confined
Her golden tresses were with band
Of azure, like the angels stand
Upon to light, each one, a star,
When Night puts up Apollo's car.
She wore a crown of evergreen
In endless wreath, in which were seen
Young buds, and blooms, and full grown leaves,
—Which ev'ry eye that sees, receives
As emblem of eternal *youth*,
In full maturity—What truth
Has writ, in part-rolled scroll, she held;
On which were thoughts so plainly spelled
That I could read. Scales, too, she bore,
And rod for measurement—no more
I needed, then, to tell her name,
Which straightway to my mem'ry came.
"Themis!" I cried, "of ancient days;
Goddess of equal words and ways;
'*Justice!*', as called in this our time,
Opponent of all fraud and crime,
I thank thee that thou dost appear
Before me: speak, and I will hear!
Just now, I heard words foul and dark:
Thou could'st not speak such—List'n, hark!
I hear a voice; but, not the same
As that whose tones so lately came."

That new voice said; "The men who dwell
In Northern States, have spirits fell.
They worship Mammon, and would sell
The rights of their best friends, as well
As make their brethren work for naught
In teeming workshops, where they ought
To find in droppings of their brow
'Good food and raiment' anyhow
For wives and children. Slaves, indeed,
Those toilers are, whose hearts do bleed,
Though *freemen* they in word are called,
By plain misnomer—falsehood bald!
Professing love for Afric's race,
Those Northern men have brought disgrace
Upon their names, by bitter hate,
Not even found in Satan's State;
—A hate of one's own race and kin.
They have outstripped the *lost* in sin;
For *Dives*, lost, did make appeal
For his five mortal brethren's weal!
That hate was shown, before the war,
In efforts Southern peace to mar,
And Southern homes with fire to burn,
And implements of death to turn
Against the whites, and to renew
The scenes of '*Saint Bartholomew.*'"

"A fiendish joy, then, hades stirr'd,
When Northern Lincoln's voice was heard
Assembling men for murd'rous deed

Upon the South, for which the meed
Of adulation he received
Throughout the North, *whilst angels grieved;*
A war those men of unjust mind
Long waged in spirit which mankind
Condemned. Their famous '*March t'ward Sea*'
Filled *Satan* with unwonted glee;
Who, welcoming the souls which fell
From out that vandal-horde to dwell
With him, said: '*You and chief have won*
THE PALM *from* ME *and* MINE! WELL DONE!!'"

"The South surrendered; then *peace* came
In outward form and spoken name,
But not in spirit; for such peace
Did but oppressive wrongs increase.
With bitter hatred, still, at heart,
The North can't do an honest part
By Southern whites; while those *they loved*
—*The poor black race*—have long since proved
What they, in other days, were told:
'*There's but one magnet, that is* GOLD,
Which can attract, and hold, and sway
The Northern heart in ev'ry way.'
There'll be a day of righteous doom,
When God will sweep with wrathful broom
Such souls, full-swayed by fraud and wrong,
Into the pit, where they belong!"

I trembled, and to Themis said:

"Heardst thou that voice with words so dread?
And didst thou hear the first which spoke
In words that fell like wrathful stroke?"
"I did," said she of heavenly birth,
"Hear both; but they are little worth.
They are the *mutt'rings of the past*
Produced anew from faithful *cast*
Of mem'ry's mystic phonograph,
At which one *now* could even laugh,
But for the fact that they contain
Some little truth to give one pain.
The phonographic wheel has been
Just now reversed by elf unseen,
To mar your pleasure in yon view *
Which Nature has displayed for you.
Those accusations were inspired
By *Prejudice* who has expired,
Or now is dying, *in dust prone,*
Where *by my order he was thrown.*
My voice, throughout this land, *is heard!*
By almost all, I am revered!
And, *North* and *South,* the *nation's throng
Confess that* THEY HAVE OFT JUDGED WRONG!"
I seized my chance, by strong wish led,
And, risking charge of rudeness, said:
"To some, a subject is involved
In *doubt* which can by *you* be solved:
'Of *sections,* which war did divide,

---

* Sunset-scene.

Which one had HONOR *on its side?'"*
She held the scales, well-poised, up high
A moment, and made this reply:
" Men, North and South, were all alike;
In war as *patriots* all did strike.
The South loved South; the North loved North;
And each loved Union, so far forth
As each esteemed it benefit.
And, hence, as South regarded it
An *injury*, she sought to break
The Union-bond: hence, too, to make
The South adhere to compact, was
Resolved upon by North; because
The Union, formed by ev'ry one
Of all the States, was priceless boon,
In her esteem, received from those
Who passed through *Revolution's throes*.
North sought *her weal*, and claimed the right
To hold in Union, South, by might.
The South claimed right, which North denied,
And for that right with vigor tried
—The right of each as 'Sov'reign State'
From Union to separate—
And in that claim, South thought she saw
Her weal, as well as right at law;
—*Her weal*, which was, of all things, most
By her desired, at any cost.
'*State*' was the *patria* revered
By *South;* while '*Union*' appeared
To *North*, alone as worth the name

Of '*Country*' which could justly claim
Alleg'ance—Thus in *honest thought
Divided*, both for *country* fought.
Hence *patriotism* was the pow'r
Which ruled them both in that sad hour,
When *Peace* was bound and rudely slain
As sacrifice to sectional gain;
—For *section* was the *country loved*
By each, *as War's red record proved*.
But now the Union doth appear
To ev'ry State as object dear;
Self-love the motive principal,
United with good-will to all.
The *multitude on either side*
The line which did this land divide
Should readily give honor due
To all '*on either side*', who threw
Themselves, their fortunes, lives—*their all!*—
On altar of what each did call
His *country; and* FEW DO *refuse*
To *honor;* FEWER still, *abuse:*
And *all* rejoice that War's rude hand
No longer waves above this land.
O, foaming streams of human blood
Need not have run like mountain-flood;
Not one man would in war have died
If ALL *had chosen* ME *as guide!*"

Into the air her form withdrew,
And quickly passed beyond my view.

But, while intent and sad I gazed
At her receding, 'round me blazed
A wondrous gleam of mellow light,
Like that oft seen on winter-night,
When thoughtless DAWN has lost his way,
And, in his consequent dismay,
Caused by the fear he may be late,
Has *erring, rushed to Northern gate;*
And, finding there his sad mistake,
Stands troubled *now* what course to take,
Then resolute, he swift turns back,
And hast'ns to his wonted track;
—Thus, *trembling,* 'round me shone the sheen,
Despite the Sun's rays, plainly seen.
It staid; and soon was steady grown;
And 'mid it, lo! a PRESENCE *shone!*—
A maid, with robe like snow,—so white;
And radiant, like the morning light,
And girt with golden cincture, set
With gems beyond all estimate!
A *torch* and gleaming *blade* she bore;
While, on her brow, a *crown* she wore.
"Are you not *Themis*," quick I said,
" Returned, with raiment changed, bright maid?
The countenance is surely hers,
As, too, the graceful form appears.
In naught you seem another, save
The raiment, torch and sword you have."
" I am not," gently she replied;
" But we are kindred close allied.

My office is to plain reveal
The errors threat'ning man's best weal
In ev'ry avenue of life,
And, also, show the good, so rife
Throughout the sphere in which man moves;
Which good, past history well proves,
Would from man's view, all lie concealed,
Were it not by my light revealed.
Her name you know; and *mine*, (forsooth,
You can by this time tell,) *is* TRUTH."

" Permit the question, why you wear
A *victor's crown*, since *Errors* share
Dominion o'er the minds of men
With you?" said I; and straightway, then
I felt that I had been quite rude
And culpable thus to obtrude
So bold a question on the maid;
And word apologetic said,
To which she mildly gave reply:
" You've done no wrong in asking why
I wear this *wreath* while Errors, bold,
A partial rule o'er man's mind hold.
*I'm crowned because where'er I go
I conquer*, tho' my march be slow.
For proof, an adage will avail,
Well known to you: '*Truth must prevail.*'
.Especially within this land
Upon whose soil we both now stand,
I have a right to wear this crown;

Which may in words, quite few, be shown :
This Continent would now be known
To aborigines alone,
Had not my *torch's* brilliant ray
Enabled one man, *far away*,
To realize its presence here,
As though his eyes beheld it near;
And cheered him 'mid discouragement
While trav'ling *Europe's* continent
For aid—and, too, while coming o'er
Atlantic's main to hither shore.
When once 'twas found, how many came
To this *'New World'!* And yet, *my flame*
Which led and cheered *Columbus*, shone
Upon the path of ev'ry one,
Across the ocean to the strand,
And *on to new homes* in *strange* land;
—As cloud, by day, and fire, by night,
To Canaan led the Israelite!"

" And your *Republic* owes to me
The fact that it *began to be!*—
And that, *to be it has not ceased*,
But *has in greatness much increased;*
—Though many dangers have been cast
Athwart its path, from first to last!
Again : 'Tis true, that to all lands
Inventions have been sent, which hands,
In this ' new world,' seized in the light
Which my torch sheds, both day and night,

And 'arts,' with untold blessings fraught,
To ply which men by *me* were taught!
Go ask the millions of this land
On what foundation, firm, do stand
The blessings which they now possess,
And hopes of others—they'll confess
Their present great prosperity,
And hope of what it yet shall be,
Are both dependent on the pow'r
Which I am wielding ev'ry hour.
The *world* is *here*, it can be said,
In *representatives:* and led
By me till useful knowledge reigns
In all their minds, and naught remains
Of ignorance to hinder sure
And rapid progress in the pure
Ennobling principles of life
Which foster peace and banish strife,
These *representatives* will go
Back whence they came, and light bestow
Upon their nations till the world
Becomes an *empire grand*, controll'd
And blessed by my benignant hand :
Then shall I reign in ev'ry land,
And *Errors* will *me* VICTOR own!
—Why should I not wear *now*, the crown?"

"Inspired by knowledge I revealed,
Men, brave, with spirits well annealed
By trials of their faith and zeal,

Have gone forth at the risk of weal,
To search in lands but little known
For gems of fact where they were strewn
By art or nature long ago;
And coming back those gems to show
And give as presents to the world,
Have gone forth yet again, and hurl'd
Into the sea huge mountains; and
Deep rivers emptied; made the sand
In quick-sands *firm; filled valleys* up;
Great lakes made *small* as baby's cup;
Hewed down vast forests (—*to use those*
Material barriers which oppose
The moving footsteps of mankind,
For checks to conquests of the mind—)
And greater treasures, still, have gained:
Nor yet have they from search refrained."

" Beneath the light which I have lent,
The land known as *'Dark Continent'*
Attracts the world's attention now;
And t'wards its shores full many a prow
Is turned by nations who do strive,
In noble contest, to derive
The profits from the largest share
Of wealth's great sources, which have there,
By Deity's creative hand,
Been placed in lake, and river, and
In mountain, and in fertile plain,
And harbors (close to rolling main

10*

Which washes south and western coasts,)
Like those of which this New World boasts."

"With pleasure I the future view,
And see the race of ebon hue
Now dwelling here in low estate
Of mental power and growth, so late
Set free from slav'ry's galling chain
—Which ne'er again will give them pain—
Returned to Afric's Continent,
Accomplished to the full extent
Of their capacity—not great—
And organized into a State
Which will illume the *Dark Domain*,
Tho', still a part will *here* remain,
To be, with men of ev'ry land,
Who shall upon this soil then stand,
Grouped as a world in min'ature,
With minds enlightened—hearts made pure—
Rich samples (fit for angels' sight!)
Of work accomplished by my light
—As growing fruits of earth do show
The pow'r of yon great Sun's bright glow."

"Thus, what I've *here* already wrought,
(Dispensing rays, which, like seeds fraught
With ample harvest yet to come,
Shall grow, until this wondrous home
Of exiles—'of the *brave* and FREE'—
Refulgent with *my light* shall be;

And shine upon earth's *moral* night,
As *Luna* shines, with *borrowed* light—)
Gives me a joy I'm proud to own
—*Entitles me to wear my crown!*"

" Alas!" said I, "that Ham's dark race
So long in bondage here—with grace
Now wearing *Freedom's golden chain*
About their necks—should not remain
Forever here, with Japheth's sons,
And Shem's (for blood of Noah runs
In all their veins the same) and show
Themselves in qualities which go
To make man noble, *equals true*
Of other men in ev'ry view:
And mingling ever side by side
With proud Caucasians, (who deride
The claim, *that races* of *dark skin*
Can be *their equals*, though *their kin*,)
Attain to highest places State
Or Church can give; and freely *mate*
In *marriage*, as their tastes incline,
With *races fair*, and thus combine
The highest qualities of all,
—*Evolving* NEW race, WORLD *will call*
'The *noblest type* of *Adam's kind*
That *can* be—*hue, physique* and *mind.*'"

" The ideal race you speak of, would
Have been produced already, could

It *ever* be—But you *appear*
Scarcely, in what you say, *sincere!*"
Said TRUTH, intently gazing, while
Her dazed appearance made me smile.
Continuing, the fair maid said:
"If Ham was black, and Shem was red
And Japheth pure (Caucasian) white,
Their children intermar'ying might
Have, (—some do think—) produced the brown
And yellow races—*not yet shown*
Superior, in any way,
Nor equal to the white; though they
Do evidently far excel
The black race; as you know full well.
Mixing of races has been tried
Quite often in this land, and wide
The mark—a *higher type*—(if set,)
Has ev'ry effort flown! Forget
Not, friend, that mingled waters flow
Not higher, but, t'ward plane below
The highest source whence streamlet springs:
—And so it is in other things.
The great Caucasian race now stands
The *first* on earth; which fact commands
Assent: 'that *greater* could not grow
From it joined with a race below.'
Still, the position you assume
Is broad enough to leave you room
To plead for privilege you claim
For Negro race: *that* the *true* aim

Of intermixing races, (brought
To lowest point of object sought,)
Is to secure a race above
The grade in which 'Ham's children' move;
And finally to lose all trace
Of black-skin and Negro race.
But this my friend cannot be done!
The white race and the black, in one
Distinct *new* race will not unite;
For, offspring will show marks (—*despite
Fond hope*,—) distinct of *this* or *that*
Race,—*white* or *black*—in broad nose, flat;
And short kinked hair; and skin quite dark;
—Or straight hair; nose and skin of mark
Caucasian. *Progeny*, indeed,
Of offspring *nearest white*, with speed
At any time, may take *black* hue,
Which nature on ancestor threw."

" Of men the races known are five:
The name of '*races*' they derive
From differentiating marks,
Quite manifold; just as the larks,
And eagles, thrushes, red-birds, crows,
And other 'races' which compose
The feathered kingdom, not *alone*
Differ, *in hue*—as is well known.
These feathered *classes* never mate
Though each class thinks itself as great

As other.   And all, ev'rywhere,
Are free to range both earth and air."

She ceased; and I, emboldened, spoke:
"Surprise I hope I'll not provoke!
—If Adam, who of *earth* was made
Was *black;* and Eve, who, it is said,
Was made of *bone,* took color *white;*
When they in marriage did unite,
Their offspring might have *yellow* been :
Hence it will readily be seen
The other races—*red* and *brown*
Would, from cross-mixing these, have grown;
Thus; *black* and *yellow, brown* produce;
And *brown* and *yellow, red*—(mis-use
Of word I've made, it may be said,
In calling copper-color, *red!*)
The *white,* and *black* might thus have *passed,*
For aye, when '*first pair*' breathed their last,
But for the fact you just, so well,
Expressed: 'Experience doth tell
That offspring, *colors may divide*
Of *parents,* or, *from either side*
Take color full; and even back
From *middle colors* take *pure black*
Or *white!*' Does not this the'ry give
A cause for *races* which now live;
And put all arguments to flight
'Gainst marriage of the *black* with *white?*
For, no *new* race *can be,* you say;

While races *old* would, in this way,
Forever be maintained, by sure
Process, in races *five*, and *pure!*"

- "How *can* this the'ry be not right?
—If first pair *both* were *black*, whence *white?*
Or if both *yellow, red,* or *brown,*
Can advent of the *rest* be shown?
If both were *white,* we find same lack
Of reason to account for *black,*
And consequently for *the rest*
(—*All offspring* of *one pair,* confessed—)
Unless an ape and human came
Into the marriage bond—(for shame!—)
The offspring taking *human shape*
Combined with *color* of the *ape;*
But can this supposition stand
The test in this enlightened land?
Do you not think this the'ry right:
'*Adam* was *black!* and *Eve* was *white?*'"

TRUTH made but short reply to this,
By which she *race-theme* did dismiss:
"That *first mankind,* female and male,
Were *both white,* nothing can avail
To controvert! The 'chosen race,'
Their direct lineage can trace
By record, back to *Eden's* '*pair*'
—*Jews* are *Caucasians,* ev'rywhere!
It matters not *how* mankind came
To be in *unlike races,* SHAME,

Upon those who amalgamate,
Imprints her brand, at any rate!
For, 'Yellow,' 'White,' 'Black,' 'Brown,' and 'Red'
Hold in *contempt* their *own* who wed
Those of another race! Which fact
Deals sure destruction, by impact,
To the assumption, that *by right*,
In marriage *races* may unite!
As I have said, Caucasian race
Is greatest now upon the face
Of earth; yet other races may
Become quite great, provided they,
Maintaining racial purity,
(Which only can give surety
Of high development of race
Peculiarities which grace
Those *grand divisions* of mankind,)
Use opportunities they find
For growth in greatness, as they move
Along the paths which God above,
Hath pointed out for them to tread
In light my *torch* and *sword* do shed!
Diversity in unity
Is shown in the community
Of men at large. How beautiful
Variety appears! How dull
Would e'en the beauteous *rainbow* seem
Were colors mixed in muddy stream!
That *each race* hath its *own career*,
Of *God appointed*, is quite clear

To me. And, therefore, should each race
With jealousy maintain its place,
By guarding its distinctive hue
With watchfulness and vigor due.
Caucasian race is *purest* known
On earth, because it does disown
Offspring, of whom, it is not sure
Both parents were Caucasians pure!
Let other races do the same ;
And trust the *future* for their *fame!*
☞ *The* WORLD'S *best weal, to well-insure,*
The RACES, *five, should be kept pure!*
Miscegenation cannot raise
The lower races! And I praise
Caucasians, that they ne'er will yield
The racial vantage which they wield
Within your land, where races meet
—As *freemen,* ALL, each other greet!
For, should Ham's children always stay
Here, *time will never be* when they
Will be the peers of Japheth's sons
—E'en of the very humblest ones—
Or occupy, in Church or State,
Positions you have styled as 'great'!
—Should e'er Caucasians fall so low
As to be level with Negro,
Then Negro will give *surest* proof
Of his *contempt ;* and *rise aloof!*
The Freedmen, here, will one day see
That though *all are,* in this land, *free,*

Yet Japheth's sons will '*man*,' and *guide*
The '*Ship of State*,' whate'er betide
—That Negro socially ne'er can
'*Move side* by *side with Caucasian*'
—That, the *new cry:* '*Away with caste*,'
Heard in the north will cease, at last!
—And, heeding Wisdom's plain command,
Those '*Sons of Ham*' to '*father-land*'
Will go; and form, as I have said,
A *State* in Africa; and shed
Light on the minds of tribes therein
With whom they are close-joined in kin!"

I dropped the theme and silent stood:
Yet, TRUTH was in such pleasant mood,
"It seems to me that *Errors* crowd
Within this land," said I, "and loud
Assert high claim, on age and youth,
To homage, *due to you*, O TRUTH!
And what they ask, each one receives
In part, at least; for man believes
What *Error* teaches—turns away
From what your presence does display:
And *Wickedness* goes hand in hand
With *Error*, through this wretched land;
While *Hopes* of good men feel the pall
Of dark *Despair* upon them fall,
Whilst yet those *Hopes* are in their prime
And buoyant at the thought, that *Time*
Has brought almost within their grasp

The objects which they reach to clasp,
—This is the hist'ry of the past,
As well as present. Do but cast
A glance upon the record made
By CRIMES, of almost ev'ry grade,
In public walks, and private life;
By ERRORS, (*noxious, thrifty, rife,*
—Like poisonous weeds 'mid growing grain;
Or, *dark, unsightly,*—like the stain
Of soot on bosom of the snow,
Or like Night's shadow on Morn's brow,)
Seen in the practice and the creed
Of Church as well as State; indeed
Of Science, Art, and what else can
Affect the rights or weal of man.
—Methinks you'll, then wear Doubt's dark frown
Upon your brow, beneath that crown!"

" While yet this nation's life and name
Were new, dark-visaged *Discord* came
To council-chamber, claimed and took
A seat whence she could overlook
The doings of the chosen few
Who met—a fact well known to you
Who, with calm *Wisdom* also, sate
Within that room, to actuate
To legislation, true and wise,
The gifted men who did comprise
The body representative,
Possessing powers the States did give.

Around that seat of *Discord*, drew
Malignant *Errors*, whom you knew;
And *Discord* could not long restrain
Her eagerness, nor did refrain
From speaking when she once began,
Until she'd thwarted ev'ry plan
By Peace suggested, which to her
At all repulsive did appear.
Those *Errors*, too, meanwhile concealed
Facts which your torch should have revealed.
Peace left the seat she occupied,
Abashed, alarmed; and just outside
The door forlorn for long time stood
Reflective, wishing that she could
To silence Discord, plan devise;
She was approached by Compromise,
Adroit of thought and speech who said
'What troubles you, O noble maid?'
She promptly then her trouble told:
Into that chamber, ardent, bold,
He entered; and—by word and look,
Accomplished what he undertook
—Drove *Discord* scowling from her seat
Into the outer world. '*Complete*,'
The vict'ry was confessed by all:
Peace smiling, entered Council-Hall;
And from the nation did arise
Loud shouts of praise to Compromise!"

"*Resolved* that *ruin should be wrought*,

DISCORD the fierce assistance sought
Of WAR—among those demons chief
Who sow the seed of human grief.
He broke the council ; with rude hand
Drove *Peace* away, and ruled the land ;
He marshalled armies ; and with sword
—A gift from Pluto—stalked abroad.
A *picture* TRUE of *his career*
Will never anywhere appear;
Unless some fallen *Raph-a-el*
Shall *paint one on* the *wall of hell,*
Assisted by some *Angelo,*
To be admired by fiends below !
He fed on human flesh ; and quaffed
From hearts as cups, hot blood ; and laughed
To see the forms and limbs of slain
And lacerated men, like grain
Sown from the hand, fly o'er the field ;
The soldier's dying groan did yield
Him music ; as aroma sweet
Th' expiring breath of youth did meet
With smile and shout from him, like flow'r
Fresh-plucked from Flora's gorgeous bow'r,
And crushed in hand, would pleasure give
To one who is compelled to live
Amid *Augean* odors ; fair
Transporting pictures by Despair,
For him, were drawn upon the face
Of wounded ; while, with mimic pace
Of fun'ral march, he mocked the wail

Of widows—But 'twill naught avail
To make an effort more to tell
Of his vile deeds, which *you* know well."

" Since War retired, Mistrust and Hate
Have held high carnival in *State,*
And in the souls on either side
The line by which War did divide
The land, and forced each part in strife
Most deadly to contend for life.
And now a gloom as dark as night
Rests on our land because through spite
A wicked wretch, his spleen to vent,
Has slain our chosen President."

" So, too, not only *here,* but *there*
And THERE *again* and EV'RYWHERE,
Injustice, rapine, fraud and *war,*
Records of men and nations, mar.
Is it not true, O Maid, despite
Thy claim, that men call each cause ' *right* '
Which *may by force of arms be won?*
That men can say ' Thy will be done!',
To God, and *then go forth to slay
Their fellow-men*—try ev'ry way
To compass their destruction; and
Above their lifeless victims stand,
And smiling say : ' *Through* GOD *we've wrought
This deed:* yes, to *their death we've brought
These prostrate forms, by just decree*

Of HEAVEN, because they would not be
Submissive to our will; *though men,*
They were—our *equal,* FELLOW-MEN !'?"

" Oft-times the wrong has fall'n before
The right upon the field of gore :
Then, plainly it to men has seemed
That *Justice* held the sword which gleamed
In triumph. But *sometimes* has *wrong*
O'er conquered right sung vict'ry's song ;
And often, when right has prevailed,
Wrongs, greater than the one assailed,
Have been made allies by the ' right '
—Have *won the vict'ry, by their might—*
Then, too, in JUSTICE' *sacred name*
Have victors waved their banners: FAME
Has placed fresh laurels on the brow
Of WAR; and men have cried, ' See how
War, righteous judgment, does accord !
—When nations disagree, the *Sword*
Gives verdict just, as though the word
Decisive, from God's throne were heard !' "

" The God to whom such praise is giv'n
For *war's results,* once came from heav'n,
And with men walked, and plainly taught
' Man's conduct should *with love* be fraught ;
Such love as each for *self* doth feel
He should *t'ward others show,* with zeal.' "

"If men possessed the same esteem
For others' rights as theirs, they'd deem
WAR, which is *now* styled '*Art sublime*'
And '*science noble,*' HEINOUS CRIME!
Then would the *evil* war has wrought
Be seen as great,—the *good* as *naught*,—
In all the hist'ry of the past,
From man's first fraticide to last!"

"In presence of such facts, fair Maid,
—Review of which I have essayed
In part—I cannot now forbear
To ask you if *your right to wear*
That VICTOR'S CROWN, *is not in doubt*
E'en to yourself? Be frank! Speak out!"
I quailed to think of what I'd said;
But grew composed as spoke the maid:
"Be calm, short-sighted mortal friend,
And closely to my words attend!
I'm well aware that sin exists;
And that vain man full oft resists
The influ'nce sent upon his mind
And heart for good; and that we find
Both *ills* and *errors* ev'rywhere
—In *other* lands, as well as *here*.
Yet much of what appears to be
Error is *man's perversity*
In doing wrong, whilst what is right
Lies full in view beneath my light.

But, come! *review* the *good* as well
As *ill* you've been so prompt to tell!"

" In ' Declaration ' which was made
Just at the nation's birth 'twas said :
'All men are equal born, and free ; '
To which the people did agree
As precious fact—yet *slavery*
Existed in the land! Now, though
Dark *Discord* did confusion throw
Upon the counsels of the land ;
And *War* did broadcast with his hand
Prolific seeds of woe; yet, *still,*
The harvest o'er, my light did fill
The minds of all, and slavery
Was driv'n away—then ' BLACKS ' *were free*
And ' WHITES ' *confessed they ought to be!*
—Was that not TROPHY *won by me?*"

" Beneath my light the people read
What one illumed by it had said :
'*Self-preservation is the first*
Great law of nature.' *Some* States burst
The bands of Union to preserve
Themselves, while *others*, to conserve
The Union, with restraining hand
Held those retiring—then the land
Was deluged with terrific flood
Of gushing, foaming human blood,
Upon whose current there were toss'd,
By myriads, mangled forms, the *cost*

Of peace which might have been *retained,*
As well as after war, *regained.*
My light shone on the while: and men,
By aid of it, saw plainly, (when
The clouds of passion passed away,)
That to preserve is not to slay;
That *no* good was by war procured
Beyond what *peace* might have secured;
While ills which followed in war's train
Were terrible—would long remain;
That tho' an evil disappeared
At end of war (when angels cheered!)
—A race from bondage was set free—
Yet THAT was plain said *not to be*
The object of the North, by those
Who ruled, and offered war to close,
And promised never to displace
A shackle from the sable race,
Provided South would but *observe*
The compact—Union Preserve—
While South the prompt reply did send:
' 'Tis not for slav'ry we contend,
But for the liberty we own
As sov'reign States—Let us alone!';
That when war closed *the States were then*
Just as before the war they'd been,
(AT PEACE, IN UNION,) and *agreed*
To *law* by which *the slaves were freed.*
Ah! then, by MOST 'twas plainly seen
'Twere better far had war not been—

*Had slaves been granted liberty
By States* which claimed full sov'reignty,
(Which States, *as now,* would *then* have found
Their weal to rest on *Union bond,*
And would have used their sov'reign pow'r
To strengthen union more and more;)
That, civil-war is suicide!
That, for the Union to divide
Might be but to destroy outright
Both *State* and *Union; to unite*
The South as *conquered* States, not *free*
And *equal with the North,* would be
As truly to break *Union*
As '*State secession*' would have done;
That 'STATES ALL EQUAL, MEN ALL FREE
Would make best Union that could be!*"

" War gave to thousands *name* and *pay*
As soldiers; pointed out the way,
For some, to Fortune's treasures, (free
To all who find them;) led with glee
The nation in a joyous whirl
Of patriotism—like the girl
Of yore, (who for her father danced,
As he, from war, t'ward home advanced,)
Indulged in. Yet not *names* and *pay*
And *Fortune's treasures,* could outweigh
The tribute laid by War upon
The nation—*part on ev'ry one;*
While Jeptha's heart was not more sad

When *Silence* hushed the voice of maid,
—*That daughter, young, to him so dear!*—
(—When she withdrew ne'er to appear
Again within his loving view,
Jephtha no deeper sorrow knew—)
Than thousands felt throughout this land
Who realized *war's stern demand!*
The *wickedness of war impressed
The nation.* Some their fears expressed:
'How can a Union gained by blood
Receive approving smile of God?'
Blood, shed in fratricidal war
Does now, indeed, with dark stain mar
This land's escutcheon—marred before
By slavery. But, as NOW o'er
*Ills which attended slavery
The nation grieves,* the time *will be*
When full confession will be made:
'*The nation sinned when it arrayed
Itself against itself; and strove
In deadly conflict,*' which did move,
In heaven and earth, the good and true
To wonder, and to pity, too!'"

"See! *All enlightened nations are
Becoming loth to enter war,*
Whene'er agreement can be made
Between those who dispute. The '*blade*'
Is dernier resort e'en now;
And some day will '*be turned to plough*'

And '*spear will change to pruning-hook*'
—As was foretold in prophet's book!"

" Good men and angels will rejoice
Ere long to hear each nation's voice
—IN CONCERT, ALL—'*We do agree
To settle questions peaceably
By means of* INTERNATIONAL COURTS,
As *man with man to law resorts.*'
THEN, *War* the *officer* will be,
IF NEEDED, *to enforce decree:*
As '*posse comitatus*', ALL
THE NATIONS will obey his call,
Whose arm will be so fierce and strong,
When once outstretched, that 'twill be long
Ere nation, afterwards, by act,
Attempt the *peace-bond to infract.*"

" Those heroes who are worshiped now,
(Whose heads beneath the sod lie low
Or, conscious of renown, with grace
Wear chaplets which the people place
Upon them, almost *daily* wove
Of praises fresh—*new buds of love*),
By future generations will
Be honored as *brave men whose skill*
Was manifested in THE ART
OF MURDER. (The conspicuous part
Performed by each, which brought him fame,
Would then be viewed as cause for shame,

But for the fact that, *charity*
Will credit the barbarity
To darkness of the soul and mind
—*Sin's shadow resting on mankind*—;
Just as the DUELLIST, *in past*
ESTEEMED, is *now* with murd'rers classed;)
War is the work of demon-mind,
Wrought through the passions of mankind :
Peace is approved of God above,
And is maintained through human love !
War brought this land unrest and toil,
Like stormful ocean has, but oil,
Which was on waters poured by Peace
Whom my light led, made unrest cease.
Now, just as yon bright setting Sun
Sends gifts alike to ev'ry one,
So do this country's blessings flow
To rich and poor, to high and low :
And as the trees and flow'rs and grass
And other growths of ev'ry class,
And stream, and rock, and barren slope,
Yea, all within his strong eye's scope,
In mutual love and peace receive
Whate'er that generous Sun does give ;
And as the smiling of the sands,
And clapping of the glad trees' hands,
And laughing of the waters' voice,
Go back to make the Sun rejoice,
So do most people in this land
In bond of mutual love now stand,

And for the blessings which are sent
Reflect their joys on Government."

"*Mistrust* and *hate* do not exist
Throughout this land, as you insist.
A few *bad men* their hatred keep :
And some *speak* hate that they may reap
A profit by their speech of ill ;
But confidence and love do fill
Most hearts of all the millions here ;—
Which doth by many proofs appear.
Yes, as they all *in this sad hour*
Feel, *each like each*, grief's crushing pow'r,
Because a devil using hand
(The only one he could command
For deed so vile) of man here found,
Has deeply pierced with painful wound
The nation's ruling Magistrate,
Beloved, as such, in ev'ry State,
So are most hearts now closely tied
By kindliness, throughout this wide
And long extending, free domain
—From Lakes to Gulf, from Main to Main.
*None love with purer love than they
Who once were foes in* 'BLUE' *and* 'GREY ';
*While o'er the graves of those who fell,
Their duty doing, bravely, well*
To NORTH or SOUTH, *the Nation stands
In grief:* and, yearly with her hands
She crowns her pallid SONS *in* 'BLUE'

And sons *in* 'GREY,' with CHAPLETS new
—Thus I have told some triumphs won
By me: and still *my light shines on!*"

" Great social battles will be fought
Within your land, when glitt'ring thought
Like polished, keen-edged, blade will be
Brandished by leaders of the free,
Pointing to where runs high the strife
Upon whose issue hangs the life
Of your Republic, or welfare
Of large communities, whose share
In Legacy of Freedom must
Defended be by *ballot*-thrust.
The minions of the demon '*Drink*'
Will press the nation's youths to brink
Of ruin, ere Sobriety
Win to her standard moiety
Of those who ballot-franchise wield.
Those *minions* may not 'quit the field,'
Yet they, throughout the land, will meet
With stunning check or full defeat.
Monopolists (—those plutocrats!—);
And social-theory-acrobats
(—The Anarchists and Nihilists—);
And every clan which now insists
On legislation for '*a class*,'
Tho' that be fondly styled '*the mass*';
Capitalists and Labor-Leagues;
And Syndicates that work intrigues

—All *these* will be controlled by *right*
Perceived by freemen through *my* light!"

" All things on earth e'en those most dark,
Possess of light the latent spark,
(Absorbed, or placed there by the Lord,)
Which friction will make blaze abroad.
E'en doth the sea drink in the rays
Which beam from sun's face through the days:
These rays afford the fishes light
In darkest hour of darkest night;
And may be seen in lustrous glow
Where vessels through the waters plow.
So, through my agency, hath Heav'n
To mankind *inward* radiance giv'n.
Tho' mind, in ignorance may seem,
Opaque, it holds a living beam:
If clothed in error's night of gloom,
Friction will make the radiance loom.
The light I shed from torch and sword
Doth to each human soul afford
Full knowledge of the honor due
To man and to the only true
And living God. And ev'rywhere,
Fruits of that knowledge now appear:
Men break their idols, give their lives
In loving, living, sacrifice
To welfare of their fellow-men,
(Thus showing love to God unseen).
Lo! fast and faster, idols fall:

And, more and more, on God men call.
My light is reaching far and wide:
And knowledge spreads like deluge tide."

" If winter-winds chant strains of woe,
And sky, sad-faced, wrap earth in snow,
And bird and beast retire, downcast,
As though earth's life were overpassed,
Yet, by-and-by, will zephyrs come,
And, folding up, bear to their home
As treasure rich, the winding-sheet
Of snow-flakes (laid in wondrous plait
By hasty hands upon Earth's form,
Cold as if dead;) and, Earth, made warm
By that same burial dress, the while,
Will ope her eyes, arise, and smile;
—Her variegated robe resume,
All redolent of sweet perfume;
Feast on repast which bounteous sun
Will spread, as he has often done,
And, strengthened thus, her work renew,
(—Present to bird's, beast's, man's glad view
Rich fruits and flowers wrought by her skill)
And say: '*Behold! I'm living still!*'"

" Tho' clouds may veil the face of morn;
And *Day* may wear a look forlorn,
And hide her face in lap of *Night*
And weep because the wonted light
Is absent from the scenes she views,

Whilst she her chosen path pursues,
Yet, *Time* will take *Morn's* veil away;
And *Night* will lead the weeping *Day*
Into the presence of the *Sun*,
Whose beaming smile will swiftly run
With healing pow'r throughout the whole
Of his dejected *daughter's* soul;
And she will visit earth again,
And smile on mountain and on plain,
Rejoicing, *that her tear-drops shed*
Have grass and fruit and flow'r fed,
And made the hungry earth look glad,
And streams go laughing as if 'mad.'
—Like manna which in darkness fell
Fed Israel, as your Scriptures tell."

"So too, tho' *Errors* do surround
My path; tho' *Evils* do abound;
Tho' *Devils* strive to quench my light,
While *Satan*, watching with keen sight
From porch in front of open door
Of lurid palace, casts all o'er
The moral world his shadow dark,
Yet, in due time, my torch's spark
And two-edged blade will hold full sway:
Those *Errors*, all, will flee away,
And ev'ry *Evil* drop its head
Before my sword discomfited;
While *Satan*, calling *Devils* home
From ev'ry place where they may roam,

Will shut himself and them within
His palace, lit with burning sin,
—As owls and bats do all retire
When angels build their morning fire
Upon the beauteous pearly hearth
Which rests on Eastern bound of earth!"

She waved her *sword;* and lo! a *light*
Rushed from it THAN HER TORCH MORE BRIGHT!
"My *torch,*" she said, "is REASON'S FLAME;
My *sword,* THE WORD OF GOD!"
       " Your claim,"
Cried I, "to wear that *Victor's Crown*
O radiant Maid"——
    LO! SHE HAD FLOWN!

CLOSING SCENES.

Closing Scenes.

SCENE ON AN OLD BATTLE-FIELD.

I westward looked, and as I, rapt, admired
The scene, the *Sun*, with princely mien, retired
Adown the jasper steps at base of which
His palace stands, in gem adornments rich.
And when into his chamber he had passed,
Then *Twilight* came to palace-dome, and cast
A monitory glance, and with her hands
Waved * into silence all these eastern lands.
Lo! Those same potent wavings brought the dead
Forth from their graves: and by the faint light shed
From beacon, which the beauteous *Venus*,† holds
In turn with *Mercury*,† to light the wolds
Within the Sun's most ample palace-court,
(Where nightly many spirits pure resort,)
As priests '*in turn*' at altar close attend

* Reference is here made to the *oscillations* noticeable at twilight.
† Evening-stars.

That they the fading sacred fires may mend,
I plainly saw forms moving to and fro,
Late risen from their graves in plain below.
I knew the plain must have been battle field
Where hundreds did their lives untimely yield.
Alarmed, I quickly moved t'ward glim'ring light
Of farm-house, seeking shelter for the night.
But as I moved those airy forms moved too,
As albatrosses near a ship will do.
On either side, behind me, and before,
With equal step they moved, as in the yore
They learned in measured, martial, pace to tread,
E'er yet their names were numbered with the dead.
Soft music, like Æolian notes most clear,
Came stealing on the quiet ev'ning air.
—*Those spirits sang* in spirit-voice more sweet
Than *earthly* tones which human ears do greet.
They sang the " *sadness wrought in late passed hour,
When greatness fell before a madman's pow'r;* "
They sang a *welcome to the murdered Chief
Executive*—which filled my heart with grief,
As they anticipated his demise
Despite the prayers ascending to the skies,
They startled me with loud triumphant shout,
As joining hands, they compassed me about
In circles all concentric, and around
Me moved, while at the centre I was found,
Though I went forward constantly. Ere long,
They sang a grand apostrophizing song

To "Union Sealed with Love." *My soul was
  thrilled!*
While with the melody the air was filled;
(—It seemed the *nation*—Dead and Living—*sang!*)
And heaven's arch with wondrous echo rang.
From joining chorus *I* could not refrain;
And *shouted,* "Union Sealed with Love," *amain!*
—Those spirit-forms departed from my sight
As quickly as the lightning sheds its light!
The echo of that song died on my ears,
As gently as the rainbow disappears!

Seeking Shelter.

The distant farm-house light
  Did now no nearer seem
Than when my eager sight
  First caught its welcome gleam.
Yet on I rode with speed,
  By pleasing prospect cheered,
Till, just before my steed,
  A lustrous mist appeared.
Trembled the steed for fear!
  Speechless the rider stared
At forms—two chieftains—near,
  With sword-points crossed, prepared
For deadly conflict on
  A grassy plat beside

The road, where *mildly shone
The mist,* now spreading wide.
A pause! *then sword-points dropped:*
Promptly both warriors spoke
—*Spoke but* ONE *word* and stopped!
Then each *his own sword broke;*
Repeated spoken word;
And throwing to the ground
With force his broken sword,
Each clasped the other 'round
In fond embrace of love,
And *"BROTHER!"*, said again.
Then from the air above
Came sudden shout: *"In twain
The swords are broke!* FOR AYE
THE NORTH AND SOUTH UNITE
LOVE'S GOLDEN CHAIN, *which they
Once broke with ill-spent might!"*
Like spacious theatre
Lighted up brilliantly,
The air did then appear
Filled with gay soldiery,
Who gave applause amain,
As both the chieftains, bound
About with glit'ring chain,
(—Their swords still on the ground—)
First, *arm in arm,* went forth;
Then, turning *face* to *face,*
Moved slow apart—one *North*

One *South*—with equal pace,
Until *remote in air*
They stood; while *stretched between,*
That golden cable (—fair
True emblem—) *could be seen*
In gentle motion, swayed
By the transparent sea,
Quiv'ring AS IT CONVEYED
LOVE'S MESSAGE CONSTANTLY.
The scene was *grand!* My brute
Looked up in calm amaze.
Forgetting to be mute,
I spoke aloud in praise:
—*The curtain fell!* the play
Was stopped! and ev'ry light
Went out! th' assembly gay
Retired in haste! and *Night*
The empty play-house closed,
And walked forth in her crown,
Whose gems I ne'er supposed
Were bright as *then* they shone!

Their soft sheen illumined our path,
And lit up the fields all around.
We reaped well the rich after-math
Of beauty we constantly found,
As onward we moved through the field
Of vision with scenes ever new;
—Where ev'rything promptly did yield

Us tribute. The small gems of dew,
Like birds' eyes, from bush and from tree
　　Peeped shyly; and on stubbles lay
Like boat-lights which one may oft see
　　Close crowded at night in a bay.
Like fairies appareled in gold
　　And silver quite tastefully mixed;
Like lone shepherd watching his fold;
　　Like huge giant, sadly transfixed
With spear of his still huger foe;
　　Like *other* scenes yet, *did the fog,*
From lowlands to hills rising slow,
　　Make shrubbery seem. O'er the bog,
The coy *ignus fatuus* shone
　　Out brightly, and went out *by turn.*
" Thou *wicked* elf, *hate you us?* *None*
　　But FOE, *Jack o' Lantern would burn*
A treacherous light," plain I heard
　　A *fairy* not far from me cry:
I looked for her—nothing appeared
　　Excepting a lone *fire-fly!*
I smiled at the rude *fairy's ire,*
　　Evoked by——— *sly* FANCY's *prompt* skill;
And turned me to see if the fire
　　Was held by " Jack " o'er the bog still.
—'*Twas* NEAR me, and dazzled my sight!
　　My steed *stopped!* The *wonder* was *great!*
—*Jack's Lantern* was naught but " *The Light*
　　In the Farm-House!" My *steed stood* at *gate!*

Just as fair *Luna* to the zenith rose,
Beneath the *farmer's* roof, I found repose.
Morn gently woke me.—*Lo!* *I was* AT HOME!
—Whilst I revolved scenes through which I had
　　come,
Gay *Fancy*, presently, to me appeared,
And said: "You owe to *me* what you have heard
And seen; tho' *Truth* did furnish many a thought
Which I into my pictures gladly wrought."

FINIS.

www.ingramcontent.com/pod-product-compliance
Lightning Source LLC
Chambersburg PA
CBHW030357170426
43202CB00010B/1405